Tai Chi Made Easy

Tai Chi Made Easy

A step-by-step guide to health and relaxation

ROBERT PARRY

Photography by
Laura Wickenden

A ≡People's Medical Society BOOK

To those present in spirit.

ADVICE TO THE READER
The author, publisher and Eddison Sadd Editions cannot accept any responsibility for injury resulting from the practice of any of the principles and techniques set out in this book. Tai chi is an excellent way to keep fit and to stay well and is also a highly efficient means of recuperation after illness. However, this book is not intended as guidance for the treatment of serious health problems; please refer to a medical professional if you are in doubt about any aspect of your condition.

First published in the U.S. in 1997 by the People's Medical Society

Library of Congress Cataloging-in-Publication Data

Parry, Robert.
    Tai Chi made easy : step-by-step guide to health and relaxation / by Robert Parry.
       p.   cm.
    ISBN 1-882606-25-6
    1. Ch'i kung.   I. Title
    RA781.8.P37   1997
    613.7' 148—dc21   96–37162
                                       CIP

First Printing, May 1997
1 3 5 7 9 10 8 6 4 2

The People's Medical Society is a nonprofit consumer health organization dedicated to the principles of better, more responsive and less expensive medical care. Organized in 1983, the People's Medical Society puts previously unavailable medical information into the hands of consumers so that they can make informed decisions about their own health care.

Membership in the People's Medical Society is $20 a year and includes a subscription to the *People's Medical Society Newsletter.*

People's Medical Society
462 Walnut Street
Allentown, PA 18102
610-770-1670

AN EDDISON·SADD EDITION
Edited, designed and produced by
Eddison Sadd Editions Limited
St Chad's House, 148 King's Cross Road
London WC1X 9DH

Phototypeset in Garamond and Humanist 777 BT using QuarkXPress on Apple Macintosh
Origination by Rainbow Graphic Arts Ltd., Hong Kong
Printed and bound by Paramount Printing Company Ltd., Hong Kong

Contents

Introduction

Tai chi is fast becoming one of the most popular forms of fitness training in the world today – but it is not just about fitness. Tai chi is also a special way of looking at life – a path of inspiration and a guide toward relaxation and health. Daily practice will not only increase your sense of well-being and help you to deal with the stress of modern living, but will also release enormous amounts of creativity and help you to stay sharp, optimistic and alert from youth right through to old age. This may sound miraculous, but it is true! This is the reason that tai chi has stood the test of time, and that today – in homes and gardens, parks and health clubs all over the world – people from all walks of life, all ages and all levels of fitness continue to practice its slow graceful movements with as much enthusiasm and fondness as they have throughout so much of recorded history.

What Is Tai Chi?

Although it might appear to be tailor-made for dealing with the modern world and its relentless pressures, tai chi has in fact been around for a considerable length of time. With its origins rooted in ancient China, this integrated exercise system for body, mind and spirit is thought to date back as far as 3000 B.C.

The literal translation of "tai" is "big" or "great," while "chi" is translated as "ultimate energy." Tai chi, therefore, is all about generating and feeling energy through movement, the ultimate energy that powers the universe – everything from the greatest star right down to the smallest of microscopic creatures.

This book shows you how to discover and experience this kind of energy for yourself. It provides practical step-by-step instruction on how to learn a gentle yet powerful dance-like sequence called a "form," which, if practiced daily, will help you to maintain health and well-being, to stay relaxed and even to ward off some of the ravages of time. There is no expensive equipment to buy, no special clothing required. You already have everything you need – the natural chi of the body, available to you at all times; it is just a question of learning how to use it. Become part of it and you will be linking into an amazing source of energy and liberation. In fact, just by opening this book you have taken the first step on a unique journey of self-discovery that could last for the rest of your life.

But Isn't Tai Chi a Martial Art?

Yes, it is! And a very effective one, too. The martial arts flourished in China during the Middle Ages, when people blended the familiar techniques of punching, kicking and striking with the long and venerable tradition of therapeutic exercise that had developed over the centuries. To this, the medical knowledge of the energy structure of the human body was then added, and the result was the birth of what became known as "tai chi ch'uan"; many of tai chi's greatest living exponents are, in fact, martial artists of a very high caliber.

However, in recent times there has been a huge resurgence of interest in the original principles of energy flow that underlie tai chi, and this has led many people, drawn by tai chi's inherent grace and beauty, to explore once again its healing and inspirational qualities. It is this very factor that is the motivation behind this book.

The Short Yang Form

This book deals in depth with one of the most popular and easy-to-learn styles of tai chi – the short yang form, named after its founder Yang Lu Chuan. This is a simplified version of one of the more traditional forms that developed in China during the eighteenth and nineteenth centuries. The short form was in fact created in the first half of the twentieth century by Master Cheng Man-ch'ing (1900–1975) – a truly remarkable man who was not only a superb exponent of tai chi, but also a professor of literature, an expert in the use of Chinese herbs, a poet, a calligrapher and a painter. His condensed version of the yang style of tai chi, developed to suit his own busy schedule, has been his greatest gift to the world.

However, many of the movements, based on the observation of animals, are of considerable antiquity: for example, Crane Spreads Its Wings. There are cave paintings depicting similar exercises dating from 200 B.C., while the legendary Yellow Emperor of China is said to have practiced exercises for health based on the movements of animals as far back as 2700 B.C. Some of the movements have less elaborate, "handed-down" names that are more self-explanatory in nature, having been attributed to the movements over the centuries through their use between teacher and pupil: for example, Turn and Cross Hands or Ward Off Left.

The Fresh Approach

Whether you learn tai chi in a class situation from a teacher or whether you choose to learn the basics from a book first and then perhaps take it further with some private study at a later date, the method of learning is usually the same and has not altered much throughout the ages. The student begins by assimilating each of the basic individual movements, one at a time, and then, once he or she is familiar with them, puts them all together to create the beautiful flowing sequence that most of us recognize as typical of tai chi. This book continues in that tradition – but it also contains some exciting new departures.

In the past, one of the difficulties a beginner would typically encounter when looking at photographs of the form was that they would all tend to present a bewildering similarity after only just a few moments of study. Here the sequence itself is divided into eight clearly defined lessons, whereas traditionally it is taught only in two parts. This results in a clear, step-by-step approach, with easy "bite-sized" chunks of the form that can be absorbed before going on to the next stage. Each lesson focuses on different aspects of movement, beginning with balance and mastering basic stances, through to moving backward and sideways, twisting and turning, and finally integrating all the skills you have learned to achieve a combination of agility, strength and grace.

Also, the sequence is demonstrated by two experienced students of tai chi – one male and one female – and this helps to differentiate between the sections, so aiding the learning process.

Each stance is illustrated by a large-scale photograph, and there are also small-scale photographs showing the front view of a position where helpful. In addition, detailed foot diagrams indicate the required position, orientation and weight distribution for each stance, along with close-up illustrations showing the position of the hands as seen from *your* – the student's – point of view. All this ensures that the movements are easy to follow and creates a highly user-friendly book containing everything you need to get started on your tai chi journey *(see page 20 for Following the Form)*.

How Long Does It Take to Learn?

Nature does not reveal her secrets lightly; tai chi, being rooted so deeply in the natural world, requires a reasonable commitment of time and energy. You will need to practice a little every day to achieve results. The material presented in this book, however, is particularly well-suited to the modern lifestyle, the whole sequence itself taking only about eight minutes to perform, which, together with a brief warm-up session, will normally bring your commitment to around just ten minutes daily. This ten minutes will never be wasted. It will repay you over and over again in terms of health and well-being.

Although you will start to feel the benefits of practicing tai chi fairly early on, most people who study the short yang form need between six months to a year to learn it all the way through. Give yourself time to assimilate the movements properly; remember that with each lesson you will be developing your skills and encountering new types of movement, and you will find it easier if you are completely comfortable with the movements in one section before you go on to the next.

However, the learning process does not stop once you have learned the form. This is the beauty and the fascination of tai chi. There is no limit to how far it can take you, so as each hill is climbed, another even more interesting one comes into view. That's tai chi. Now give it a try!

PART ONE

Learning the Form

This part of the book concentrates on the physical side of things, the learning of the individual movements that, when added together, ultimately transform themselves into the elegant, flowing sequence known as the short yang form. The form has a beginning and an end, and whenever it is performed the movements are always repeated in the same order. It is useful to compare this to a graceful slow-motion dance or to a piece of music that always continues from its beginning to its inevitable conclusion with a constant and even tempo throughout.

Rhythm and tempo are, in fact, the keys to fluent tai chi technique. The rhythm is one we are all very familiar with: the rhythm of the breath. When we are very relaxed and calm our breathing becomes long and regularly spaced; conversely when we are excited or angry our breathing becomes rapid and irregular. In tai chi we cultivate regular breathing coupled with slow, carefully measured movements so that, in time, we become more internally balanced and harmonized with the natural world.

ONE
Getting Started

Before you learn the movements of the form, you need to be familiar with the basic principles of tai chi practice – standard foot and hand positions and things you should and should not do. This section introduces typical tai chi stances and also includes exercises for that all-important warm-up. Always wear loose, comfortable clothing and footwear that will not slide about (practice barefoot if you prefer).

Warm-up Exercises

It is always a good idea to do some warm-up exercises before your tai chi: if your joints are loose and your muscles warmed beforehand, you will get the maximum benefit from the tai chi itself. Also, if you are working outdoors, especially in cool weather, warming up ensures that you are less likely to strain your muscles or get a cramp. So here is an outline for a brief warm-up session consisting of seven simple exercises that should take no more than a couple of minutes to perform altogether. Repeat them several times if you wish.

COMPLETE STRETCH

With your knees slightly bent, spread your arms wide and lean slightly backward as you breathe in, then straighten up, bring your hands together, palms up initially (see top right), *then back-to-back as you breathe out and squat down* (see bottom right). *As you move, your hands (still back-to-back) swoop down between the knees and then part as you straighten your back again and breathe in. Open your arms wide once more as you come up and then carry on by repeating the same movement a few more times.*

11

TWISTING

With your feet and knees wide apart, gently twist your body from side to side, allowing your arms to relax and swing around as you turn. The movements come from the center of the body, not from the shoulders or arms. Relax your shoulders, and let your arms go very loose so that they wind around your body as you turn. Increase the size of the rotation by raising the opposite heel each time (your feet remain in the same position – you simply transfer your weight as you twist). All the while, make sure you keep your knees apart, as if you were sitting on a horse.

SQUATTING

Bring your palms together and then, keeping the movement as slow as you can, squat down – not too far at first – raising your heels and bending your knees as you go. Do not worry if you feel stiff to begin with; you will find that you are gradually able to increase the depth to which you can squat. You may also hear cracking from your knees – that's OK! It simply means that you are clearing out congested energy from the joints.

TURNING THE WHEEL

Squat down on one side only, stretching the other leg straight as you go. Imagine that your hands are holding an imaginary wheel as you squat down with your palms held out, relaxed and wide – not tense – and with lots of space between your arms and your body. Try to feel the work along your inside leg. Repeat this movement as desired. Then pause, bring your weight into your other foot and repeat the same number of times on the other side.

ROTATING THE HANDS

Holding your hands out in front of you with your fingers loose and pointing down, slowly rotate your hands (in opposite directions) from the wrist joint; your forearms should remain still. The rotations should be fairly slow with large movements. Then pause and continue the rotations in the reverse direction. To finish, shake your hands vigorously to really loosen them up.

ROTATING THE FEET

With a slight bend in one knee to help you balance, raise one foot and slowly rotate it from the ankle joint. Again, try to make these rotations as large as possible and rotate in both directions. Your knee should remain still. Then shake or kick out gently with the foot for a few moments to really loosen it before lowering it slowly to the ground. Reverse sides, repeat roughly the same number of rotations with your other foot and shake out again to finish.

ROCKING ON HEELS AND TOES

With a good bend to the knees, swing your arms and allow your body to rock very gently back and forth by raising both heels as you rock forward, and raising the toes of both feet as you rock backward. Again, the movement comes from the center of the body, so keep those shoulders relaxed! Also, note how the hands rotate during each swing so that the palms are always turned up at the finish, front and back, providing extra rotations for those all-important wrist joints.

Basic Stances and Hand Work

Before we explore the tai chi movements in detail we need to take a brief look at some of the typical stances and hand shapes involved. It is worth taking a little time to understand these basic principles before attempting to study the form itself. Knowing them will make the learning process much easier and will also help you to avoid developing any bad habits later on.

NARROW STANCES

A narrow stance means that most of your weight (90%) is in your rear leg, with either the toes of the front foot (a narrow toe stance) or the heel of the front foot (a narrow heel stance) in light contact with the ground ahead of you. In both cases the front foot is roughly in line with the edge of the back heel.

THE WIDE 70/30 STANCE

"70/30" refers to the ratio of weight between the feet, with roughly 70% in one leg and 30% in the other. The greater part of your weight can be either forward in the front leg or back in the rear leg. The term "wide" means the width across your shoulders from tip to tip. In 70/30 stances you always strive to keep this amount of space between your feet, regardless of the distance between the front and the back foot (therefore, when seen from the front the feet should always be shoulder-width apart). It is rather like standing on railroad tracks – admittedly a rather narrow-gauge railroad, but the principle is the same.

HOLDING THE BALL

When learning many of the tai chi movements it is often helpful to visualize a ball being held in various ways between your hands. This ensures a good energy connection between the palms which, in time, you will begin to feel. Of course, the ball itself does not always have to be strictly spherical in shape; sometimes it becomes stretched or compressed, and at others small or large. This principle of communication between the hands and arms continues throughout almost the entire form.

CUPPING THE ELBOW

This is a configuration that appears quite often in various guises throughout the tai chi form. Here you do not literally cup or support the elbow in any physical sense; rather, the palm is a good distance from the elbow itself and roughly in line with the vital center of your body situated in your abdomen: in China this is known as the Tan Tien *and in Japan as the* Hara *(see also overleaf). The fingers of the lower hand are always relaxed, while the top hand can be either flat in shape, as shown here, or gently curved over.*

PALM HAND

This is the kind of hand shape you would use if you were pushing or striking out at something with your palms. It can be done with either one hand or both together, as shown left. The fingers remain gently curved. Keep your elbows away from your sides when you push, allowing your breath and chi to flow smoothly through your chest and shoulders. You should focus in part on the Neigung, *an important energy point in the center of the palm.*

FLAT HAND

Here the fingers straighten out to give a flattened appearance (see right). It is not often encountered, but when it is, it must not become a source of tension. Although the fingers are fairly straight compared to most tai chi movements, they should not become rigid and stiff. This allows the chi to keep flowing from the shoulders right to the fingertips.

15

Dos and Don'ts

In order for the vital energy to flow unimpeded through the entire body, you need to keep your spine and limbs correctly aligned and your joints open and loose. The following advice will help you to maintain this proper alignment during your tai chi practice. It is worth referring to this section occasionally, even when you feel you have learned the form thoroughly. In times of doubt or whenever you suspect your tai chi is not flowing smoothly, check you are not doing something fundamentally wrong to upset your equilibrium.

KEEP THE SPINE UPRIGHT

Traditionally when we learn tai chi we are told to imagine a point of suspension situated on the crown of the head. From this, a golden thread goes up to the heavens, so that we move as if suspended, always vertical. Another way to think of this is to compare the base of the spine to the bob on the end of a plumb line. No matter whether the plumb line moves forward or back, the string always remains upright.

NEVER TIGHTLY LOCK THE ELBOWS OR KNEES

This rule also goes for all the joints in the body. A useful analogy here is to think of water in a hose. When the hose has a twist in it or a tight bend, the water ceases to flow smoothly or may stop altogether; the same applies to the chi in the body. So try to maintain a relaxed and flexible look to the limbs, without tension. This, again, enables the blood and other vital fluids of the body to flow easily and without obstruction. You will notice that a quality of openness and space can be seen in all the photographs featured in this book; this is particularly important in tai chi.

MOVE FROM THE CENTER

Our vital energy center is situated in the abdomen – it is a point just below the navel called the Tan Tien. *In tai chi all of the turns, steps and rotations should be directed from here – like a searchlight guiding the movements of the limbs. We also try to direct our breathing down into that area; even though the air itself obviously goes to the lungs, we still imagine the essence of the breath sinking to the Tan Tien, a constant focus of attention. Try to retain this quality of self-awareness throughout your tai chi practice.*

MAINTAIN A LOW CENTER OF GRAVITY

When you do your tai chi always allow your weight to sink down. A slight bend to the knees helps to create the typical tai chi appearance, which is somewhat low-slung and stealth-like. This characteristic should be cultivated during all of your work so that the movements flow one into the other without bobbing up or down. If you look closely you will see that in almost all of the stances shown in this book, the knees have a considerable bend to them.

DROP THE SHOULDERS

This is not always easy for those who suffer from stress because the shoulders tend to collect tension very easily – and then surrender it only very grudgingly, despite our best efforts! However, tai chi provides an excellent opportunity to correct bad habits and to dispel areas of accustomed tension. Therefore, as your arms move, and especially as they rise, try not to let your shoulders rise up with them. If you do allow your shoulders to rise, this will result in the incorrect posture shown to the left. The correct posture is shown to the right.

KEEP SPACE BETWEEN YOUR ARMS AND YOUR BODY

In tai chi there is always a generous amount of space under the arms, leaving the armpits with an open feeling. Also, the elbows do not come into contact with the sides at any time, as shown far left. All this frees the chest and rib cage; it allows you to breathe more easily and encourages the energy to flow more smoothly along the arms. Do not overdo this, though – we are not seeking the "gorilla" look here! You simply need to adopt a posture of openness and relaxation.

STEP FORWARD HEEL FIRST

Always step forward making contact with the heel first (see right) and not the toes (see left). Conversely, when you step back your toes should make contact first. This ensures a smooth action and is, in fact, the way the legs like to unbend naturally, with the least number of adjustments among the joints. Also, after any step forward always be ready to adjust the back foot to a comfortable position by pivoting a little on the back heel; if your heel will not turn, and you can only pivot on the ball of your foot, there is usually one simple explanation: you have stepped too narrow.

FRONT KNEE OVER TOES

In wide stances, when you bring your weight forward make sure the knee does not extend beyond the toes on the front foot. This would only create instability in your stance (see far left). Rather, always try to keep the knee and toes in alignment (see left); for most of us, because of the line-of-sight effect, the toes should just disappear beneath the knee as you look down.

KEEP THE KNEE ABOVE THE FRONT FOOT

In wide stances, make sure that your knee remains above what is called the "substantial" foot – the one carrying the weight – and is not turned or twisted inward (see left). Rather, always try to keep your thigh, knee, shin and foot in line (see right); weakness of the energies that flow along the inside of the leg can be responsible for any difficulty in achieving this position. Try to be aware of this and correct it by spiraling the knee back over the foot.

DON'T STAND TOO NARROW

Narrow stances should not be too narrow, as shown far left. As a rule, the front foot should always be roughly in a line with the edge of the back heel and not too close to it in terms of length either (see left). Try to be generous with this type of stance and make sure that the thigh, knee, shin and foot are all aligned so that your foot does not protrude to the side in a twisted fashion. Try not to introduce any unnecessary tension by raising the heels or toes too much.

Following the Form

Once you are familiar with the basic stances and principles, you are ready to begin learning the form itself. All the movements are clearly illustrated with photographs showing both the yin phase (the "yielding" aspect that accompanies the in-breath) and the yang phase (the "thrust" of the movement that accompanies the out-breath). If you pay close attention to the positions shown and read the instructions carefully, you will find it easy to follow the movements yourself. Remember – be patient. Learn each section thoroughly before going on to the next and think in terms of months rather than weeks for learning the form all the way through.

Although the entire sequence should take around eight minutes to perform, it can be done more slowly if you wish. Beginners tend to be a little faster than the more advanced students, although Master Cheng himself used to do it in five minutes or less! The main thing is to feel relaxed with what you are doing, and bear in mind that extreme slowness can introduce more tension than it removes. Find your own pace and let this take you wherever you need to go.

Foot and Hand Positions

On the foot diagrams the foot bearing the higher percentage of weight is labeled. The shaded area indicates the part of the foot in contact with the ground. Against these diagrams you will find the cardinal directions of north, south, east and west (except for the stances involved in moving from one direction to another). These are traditionally used by tai chi teachers to help students find the correct orientation; here they are given as a guide only to help with the learning process. In practice, this is preferable to continually referring to left and right, which can become confusing. You do not literally have to face these directions. When dotted lines are shown, these indicate a change of position – that a step has taken place: the dots show the location of the previous stance.

The hands are only illustrated when they are within your field of vision; there are, therefore, occasions when only one hand is illustrated or when neither hand is shown. These illustrations help to ensure not only that are you looking in the right direction, but also that your hands are as they should be, since the hand positions may not always be easy to see in the photograph.

Breathing

Each movement is accompanied by instructions for breathing: do not force yourself to follow these if you feel at all uncomfortable. Begin by finding your own rhythm of inhalation and exhalation; you will gradually begin to tune in to the breathing patterns given. Remember that in tai chi the learning process should always be one of discovery and fun. Relax and enjoy it!

A Deeper Level

Tai chi has a strong mental and even spiritual aspect. It is not essential for you to explore these areas in order to obtain the wonderful benefits that tai chi can bring in terms of physical health and relaxation, but they will help you find satisfaction and enjoyment in what you are doing.

It all comes down to understanding the original concept of the universal "Tai Chi," the supreme ultimate energy often depicted as a circle divided by a graceful curve (the *Tai Chi Tu* – the yin–yang symbol), suggesting movement and change. "Change" is the key word. The light half of the circle is yang, the dark half yin; these two forces, the positive and negative forces of nature, balance and complement each other perfectly in a state of continual harmony. Each one nourishes and supports the other in a perpetual rhythm of change.

Translated into physical movement, this gives us the tai chi form, which alternates constantly between negative and positive forces, accompanied by the in-breath (yin) and the out-breath (yang), so that the changes take place at a very deep level. These ideas are explored more fully in Part Two. For now, be aware that your tai chi is a reflection and celebration of nature, of great universal forces and rhythms with which we can work in harmony to benefit ourselves, not only physically but mentally and emotionally as well.

TWO

The Early Moves

The early movements of the form are all about developing balance and becoming aware of your own personal space. Wide 70/30 stances are featured heavily in this section, so always keep in mind those "railroad tracks" mentioned on page 14 – your feet should be shoulder-width apart when you step, regardless of the distance between one foot and the other.

Preparation

Master Cheng Man-ch'ing described this posture as representing the primordial state of the universe, the great "Tai Chi" before it separates into the polarities of yang and yin. It becomes, therefore, a moment of meditation with the whole body feeling relaxed and natural.

50%

50%

1 *Breathe In*
Face south to begin, your back straight and shoulders relaxed. Make sure that you are not leaning forward, backward or to one side. Your hips should be level, and your arms should hang loosely by your sides rather than being pressed close to your body. Keep your buttocks tucked in and your neck straight by tucking in your chin a little. Then slowly, empty your weight from your left side and allow your left foot to lift and then slide out to the left.

2 *Breathe Out*
Set your left foot down shoulder-width from your right with your toes pointing south, then adjust your right toes to also point south just before allowing your weight to settle evenly into both feet. Relax and imagine your weight sinking down. Keep your back straight, not leaning forward, not leaning back. Think of the plumb line *(see page 16)* and allow your spine to hang perfectly vertically, as if it were suspended from above.

Opening

Those who work long hours at keyboards will realize the importance of these next relatively simple movements, because tense hands and fingers tend to *tremble when you move them slowly. This humble little sequence is in fact a valuable relaxation exercise for the fingers and wrist joints.*

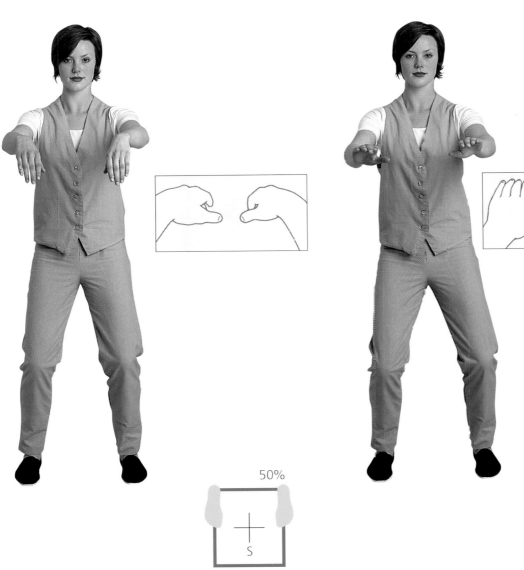

50%

50%

3 *Breathe In*
With your wrists and fingers loose, raise your forearms, as if floating in water, until they become roughly parallel to the ground. Take care that your shoulders do not rise up as well – this would only introduce tension. Be aware of how even these fairly simple movements might affect other parts of the body: the loose wrists, for example, tell your body right away that you intend to relax your arms. All this makes a difference in the way you feel about the movements.

4 *Breathe Out*
Slowly straighten your fingers. Imagine the energy coming from between your shoulders to straighten your fingers as you exhale. As you do this, however, make sure your palms do not lift or appear to push forward. In this instance, it is sometimes more helpful to think of the wrists *dropping* rather than the fingers rising. Dropping the wrists is a "letting go" kind of movement, which is preferable to the more tensile operation involved in raising the fingers.

Opening (continued)

You can actually repeat this brief opening sequence of raising and lowering the arms as often as you wish – especially if you feel it helps you to relax and adjust to the slow rhythm of movement required for the rest of the form. Beginners often find this very helpful.

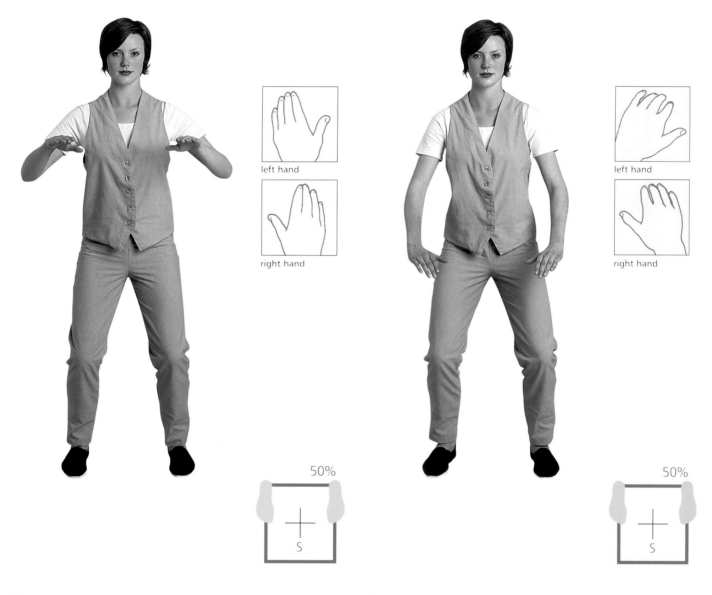

left hand

right hand

50%

S

left hand

right hand

50%

S

5 *Breathe In*
Draw your elbows back a little – not too far, otherwise the area between your shoulder blades could become tense. Do not lean back as your elbows withdraw; only your arms should move. Also, make sure you keep space between your arms and sides. This allows the breath to flow easily in the chest and is part of the whole concept of recognizing your own personal space. Make room for yourself! Remember that tai chi works on all levels: physical, mental and emotional.

6 *Breathe Out*
Lower your arms and sink down, letting your knees bend a little more. Relax your shoulders, chest and arms, and imagine your weight sinking into the ground. Think of pushing a ball down through water as you do this, although remember – whenever you hear the word "push" in tai chi, it is always meant to be without muscular tension with the arms remaining light at all times. Continue to keep that straight back. Bear in mind that sinking down is not the same as leaning forward. *Never* lean.

Turn Right

For those with stiff knees or who – at this early stage – might find it difficult to get the foot right around ninety degrees, don't worry! Just turn as far as is *comfortable and then set your foot down. In time you will become more flexible, and your knees will be able to let your feet follow the indicated position.*

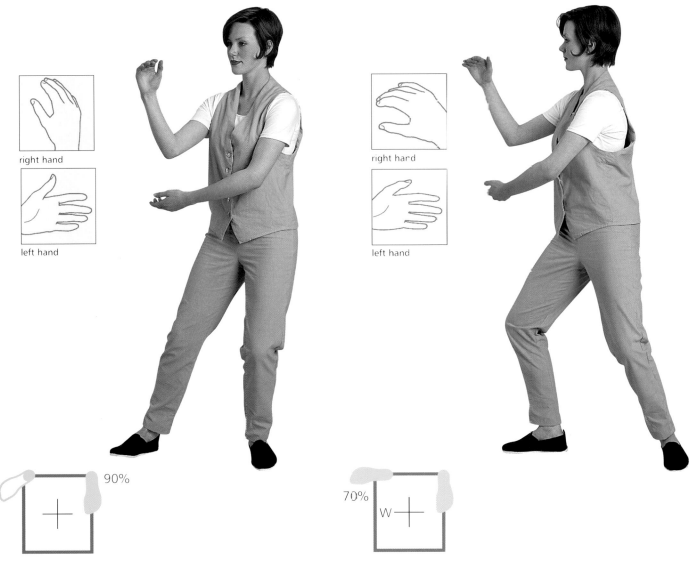

right hand

left hand

90%

right hand

left hand

70%

W

7 *Breathe In*
Empty the weight from your right side by sinking into your left foot. Then slowly pivot on your right heel to point your toes west. At the same time raise your right forearm and begin to cup your right elbow with your left palm as your waist turns toward the right; your right hand should be loosely curved. Remember the terminology here: in cupping the elbow *(see page 15)* the hand does not literally make contact with the elbow or support it in any physical sense.

8 *Breathe Out*
Bend your right knee to align with the tip of your foot. You might find that your left knee wants to bend a little too. Let it go. Relax! By now, your head, hips and shoulders have turned toward the west, and your hands have moved position slightly so that they are holding an imaginary ball – the right hand curved over on top of the ball and the left hand supporting the ball from underneath. Meanwhile your gaze becomes directed outward, looking just over your right hand, as if toward a far-off horizon.

Ward Off

During the Ward Off, the hands do what is some-times called "palming" – that is, the surfaces of both palms figuratively "stroke" each other at a distance, one rising as the other falls. The subtle energy connection between the hands, which you should eventually feel, is therefore maintained.

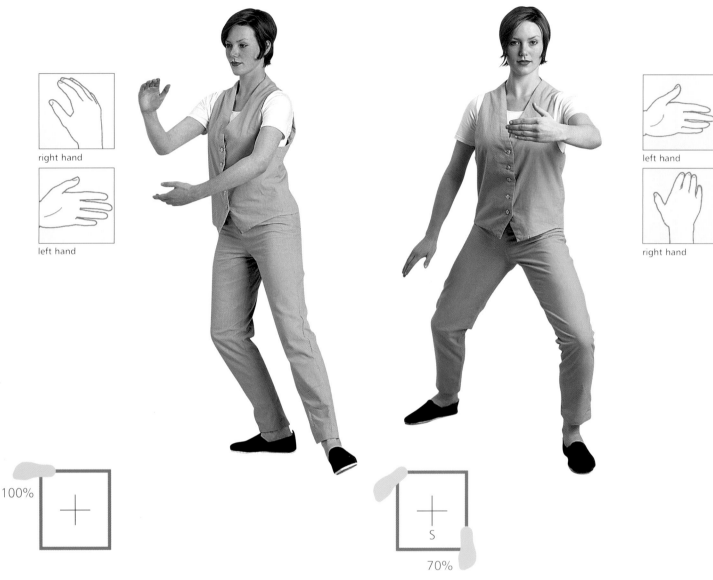

right hand

left hand

100%

left hand

right hand

70%

S

9 *Breathe In*
Prepare to step ahead, toward the south, by bringing all your weight into your right leg and draw-ing in your left toes just a little toward your right heel. This drawing in of the toes is a typical preparation for moving into a wide stance and helps to test your bal-ance before stepping – which you will do in a moment by extending your left leg out toward the south. At this stage, the right palm turns just a little forward, ready to "stroke" downward.

10 *Breathe Out*
Step forward with your left foot and turn your waist toward the south so that your center is facing forward. This is the first of our 70/30 stances *(see page 14)*, so you will need to place your foot outward good and wide. At the same time your left arm rises, the forearm horizontal, palm facing in toward the chest, while your right hand drops to the side. Finally, pivot inward a little on your right heel, to release any tension in the back knee.

Grasp the Bird's Tail

Often during the form certain movements are repeated, and here the repetitions occur in a brief sequence all their own. Using the analogy of tai chi as a piece of music, we can call this sequence the "Chorus." *It occurs four times in all, and the rest of this section is devoted to showing it in detail. Note that despite the name of this movement, the hands do not "grasp" anything – keep them relaxed throughout.*

left hand

right hand

left hand

right hand

100%

90%

70%

11 *Breathe In*
Begin by turning your waist slightly to the left and then pick up another imaginary ball, this time with the left hand on top. Empty the weight from your right side and prepare to step by drawing in your right toes a little toward your left heel. It is worth noting that the image of the "ball" here, as elsewhere, is just to get you started; these movements will soon feel natural on their own.

11a *In-breath Finishes*
Sink into your left leg, lift your right foot from the ground and, turning your waist clockwise, step around to the west, heel first. Meanwhile, the ball goes with you, the in-breath is completed, and your heel actually makes contact with the ground just as the out-breath begins. Notice how the fingers of the left hand become more upright as the heel touches back down.

12 *Breathe Out*
Bend your right knee to bring your weight forward and adjust your back heel to a comfortable position. The imaginary ball has closed up by this time, and you finish with your right arm slanting upward at a gentle angle and the fingers of your left hand pointing at the right palm. Now imagine holding a bird in your right palm, while your left hand rests on the long tail feathers behind.

27

Rollback and Press

There is no need to lift the feet at all during the next few movements. Instead, your weight changes smoothly back and forth between the front and back legs. Try to resist the temptation to raise your toes and heels as you do this; rather, your feet should remain firmly rooted, flat on the ground.

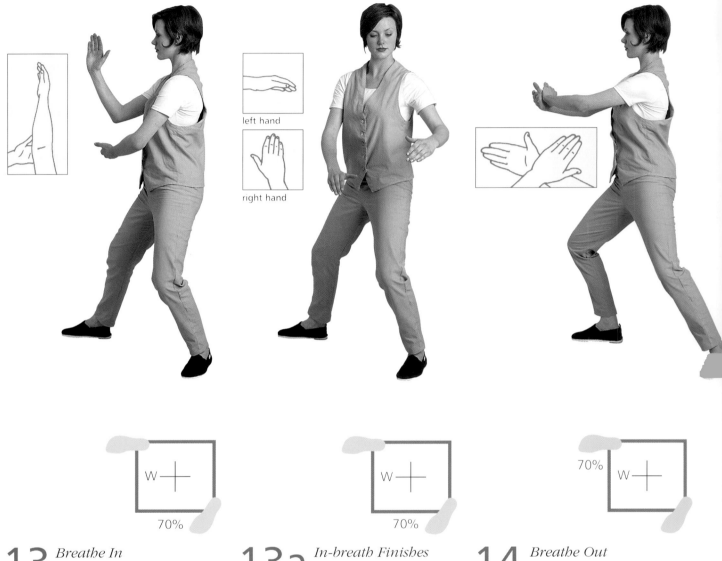

left hand

right hand

W+

70%

W+

70%

70%

W+

13 *Breathe In*
Begin by shifting your weight into the back leg. Rotate your hands slightly as you "slide" your left hand down your right forearm at a distance to cup your right elbow. The angle at the elbow becomes a little more acute as your right hand flattens out. Meanwhile, your waist turns ever so slightly to the right. Make sure your left arm does not crowd in on your center.

13a *In-breath Finishes*
Turn your waist counterclockwise and circle your left hand back behind you, while your right forearm folds down across your center. Most of your weight is now in the back leg, and your left hand is fairly relaxed compared to the right. Try to cultivate a feeling of contact between the palms as you go through this maneuver, as if you can sense the energetic connection between the hands.

14 *Breathe Out*
Rotate your palms to face each other, then bend your right knee and turn your waist back toward the west. As you return your weight to your right side, allow your left palm to approach the right until the heels of the palms (the fleshy part at the base) make contact in front of your chest. Most of the hand energy is now concentrated in your left hand to mirror the energy of the right leg.

28

Separate Hands and Push

This movement is repeated several times in the form, and a common error is to lean, either backward, as if recoiling in shock, or forward, as if leaning upon a heavy object. Instead, whenever you feel the urge to lean or whenever you suspect that you might be leaning, sink downward.

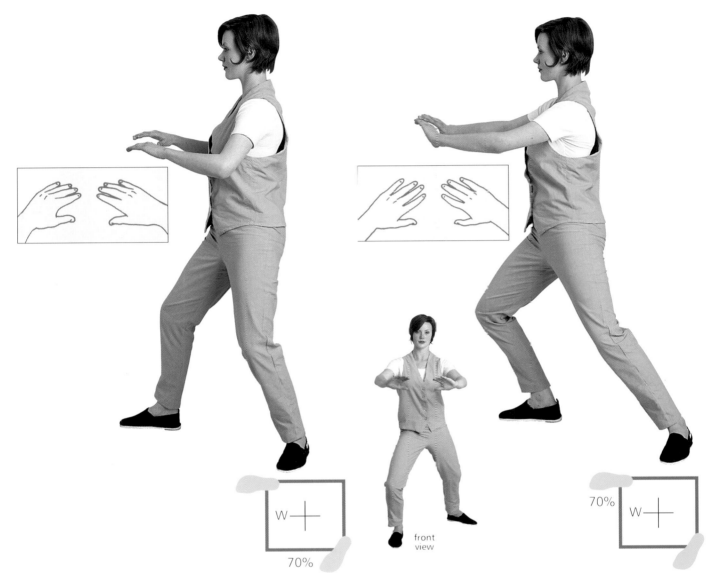

front
view

W

70%

70%

W

15 *Breathe In*
Rotate your hands so that your palms are facing downward, then separate them outward and back with a little swimming motion as you sit back once again into the rear leg, making sure that you do not lock the front knee as you go. Your hands should be relaxed with your thumbs pointing toward the sides of the chest – rather like a man about to tuck them into his suspenders – although do not overdo this. As always, you should aim to create a relaxed appearance to the movement, as opposed to a contrived or artificial one.

16 *Breathe Out*
Rotate your palms into a pushing position and then return your weight slowly forward by bending your right knee. Your hands should be covering the center of your body, rather than spread out to the sides, with your thumbs almost pointing toward each other; this helps to take the elbows away from the sides and enables the breath and the chi to flow comfortably in the chest. Your shoulders and arms should not tense up or travel any great distance during this movement; the "push" comes from the legs – the bending of the knees, not the arms. Remember, too, not to lean forward with the push; keep your back straight.

29

Single Whip

Again we have an important movement that is repeated several times in the tai chi form – the Single Whip. This is a wonderful toning exercise for the waist, featuring lots of gentle turning and twisting. Students often wonder about the feet needing *to become pigeon-toed like this – it can seem so uncomfortable! In fact, it helps us to find the root, the sense of being connected firmly to the ground. Try to keep your knees apart, and in time the whole movement will feel perfectly natural.*

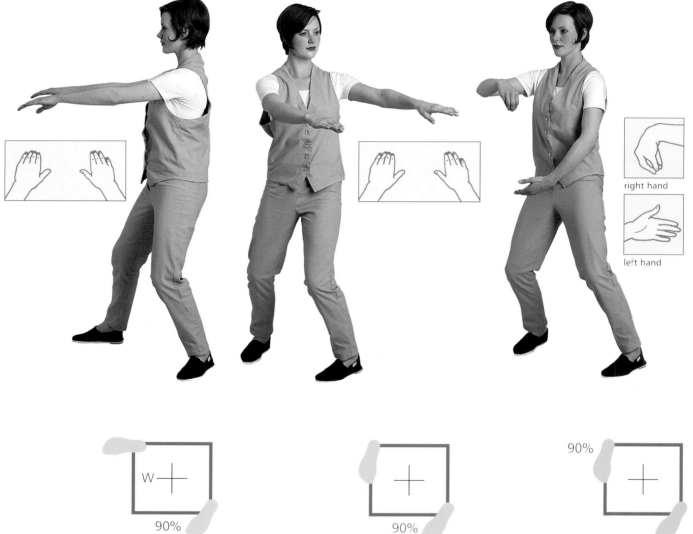

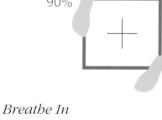

right hand

left hand

17 *Breathe In*
Sit back on the rear leg and allow your arms to straighten, though not so far as to lock the elbows, which you never do in tai chi. Your palms should be facing down. Do not straighten your arms by "diving" forward; all you need to do is keep your arms relaxed and in the same place as they were at the end of the push. As you sit back they will automatically straighten for you. Tai chi is without effort.

18 *Breathe Out*
With the weight mostly in your left side, pivot very slowly on your right heel to turn your waist counterclockwise, allowing your arms to follow your center as your waist turns around. Do not go so far as to feel "wound up"; remember that all these movements should feel comfortable and agreeable. The feet become slightly pigeon-toed, pointing in toward each other as if on the sides of a triangle.

19 *Breathe In*
Your waist now reverses direction, rotating clockwise, while your right hand is drawn across near to your right shoulder, forming a "crane's beak" – a hook shape with the fingers and thumb lightly touching. Meanwhile, your left hand swoops down, palm up, to settle near your right hip, as though to support a balloon from beneath, with the fingers of the right hand "pinching" the neck of the balloon.

30

Single Whip (continued)

The name "Single Whip" may seem peculiar, but it derives from a somewhat more intricate version found in the traditional long form of yang tai chi, in which the extension of the arm does indeed resemble the rippling movements of a whipcord. Although this "whipping" motion is no longer apparent in the short form, the name has remained the same to this day.

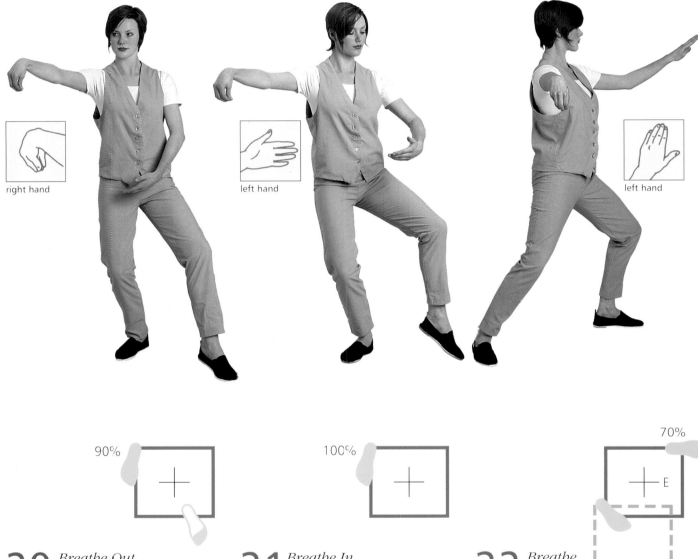

right hand

left hand

left hand

90%

100%

70%

E

20 *Breathe Out*
With most of your weight now in your right side, raise your left heel and pivot on your toes, turning your waist counterclockwise as you do so. At the same time, straighten your right arm (without locking your elbow) to project your crane's beak toward the southwest, your gaze following your right hand. These movements encourage flexibility and relaxation in the wrists and elbows.

21 *Breathe In*
For the final stage, empty all the weight from your left side and prepare to step around with your left heel to the east. Your left hand rises at this point, palm facing in; look at your palm as it rises to ensure the correct orientation of the arm. Let your elbow *float*. Sink your weight into your right foot as you do this; then, when you feel balanced, draw your left toes in toward your right heel, ready to step.

22 *Breathe Out*
Step around to the east with your left heel and bend your knee. As soon as the weight returns to your left side, pivot on your right heel to adjust your back foot to a comfortable position. Meanwhile, your left hand rotates to point the fingers outward. It should be lined up with the left side of the chest (*see step 56 for front view*). The crane's beak remains a continual focus of energy.

31

THREE

Introducing Narrow Stances

In this section we meet with the narrow stances *(see page 14)* in which most of the weight goes into the rear leg, with either the heel or the toes of the front foot in light contact with the ground. The focus here, therefore, is on developing greater balance, both physically and mentally. Narrow stances are also an excellent preparation for the kicking sequences that occur later in the form.

Play Guitar

The name Play Guitar is one that is best not taken too literally. Anyone who has ever played this instrument will realize that the configuration of the arms is not in the least bit like playing a guitar!

However, the fingers of the left hand do curve inward, rather like strumming an instrument of some kind, and this is perhaps where the name can be helpful.

left hand

left hand

right hand

90%

90%

90%

S

23 *Breathe In*
From the Single Whip, the point at which you finished the previous section, you now come to a movement called Play Guitar – a narrow heel stance to the south. Begin by letting go of the crane's beak in your right hand, relax your arms and turn your left toes in slightly by pivoting on your left heel. The left hand changes shape a little with this, just as you commence your inhalation.

23a *In-breath Finishes*
Now shift your weight entirely into your left leg, keeping the knee bent and soft. Rotate your waist a little toward the south (clockwise) and prepare for the final stage of the movement by raising your right heel, ready to draw your foot across in front of you. Although at this point your right toes may still be in contact with the ground, they should be carrying hardly any weight.

24 *Breathe Out*
Lift up your toes and draw your right heel across to place it down in a narrow heel stance, hips and shoulders facing south. Your hands, meanwhile, close in toward each other, your right arm extended a little further in front of you than your left, until you finish with the palm of the left hand facing your right forearm. Try to feel the energetic connection between your arms as they approach each other.

Pull and Step With Shoulder

The most common error in Step With Shoulder is to lean forward with the final step. Also, the right knee has a tendency to turn in as the waist rotates, *resulting in a twisted look. To remedy this, at the end of the movement try to keep your right knee spiraled outward, clockwise, above your right foot.*

90%

70%

25 *Breathe In*
Lower your arms, rather like pulling a thick rope downward with your hands – your left hand near your left hip, your right arm across your center, almost vertical. Simultaneously draw in your right toes to place them just ahead of your left heel (this is about as close as the two feet ever come to each other in tai chi); your waist turns slightly counterclockwise as you do this. Do not forget to leave some space – even here – between your arms and your body.

26 *Breathe Out*
Step wide with the right foot, transferring your weight, and rotate your waist a little more to your left as you go, so that your right shoulder appears to project forward – similar to someone breaking in through a door. Your right arm stays where it was in the previous stance, but your left hand rises a little, roughly to the height of your lower ribs, palm slightly forward-facing but still maintaining a subtle energy connection with the right forearm. Because of the twist to the waist, the hips and shoulders face southeast at the finish.

Crane Spreads Its Wings

The crane is an important creature in oriental reckoning since it exemplifies the two great qualities of strength and grace – a rare combination, but one toward which the tai chi student should always aspire. The extent to which these qualities have been reconciled in daily life is also quite revealing.

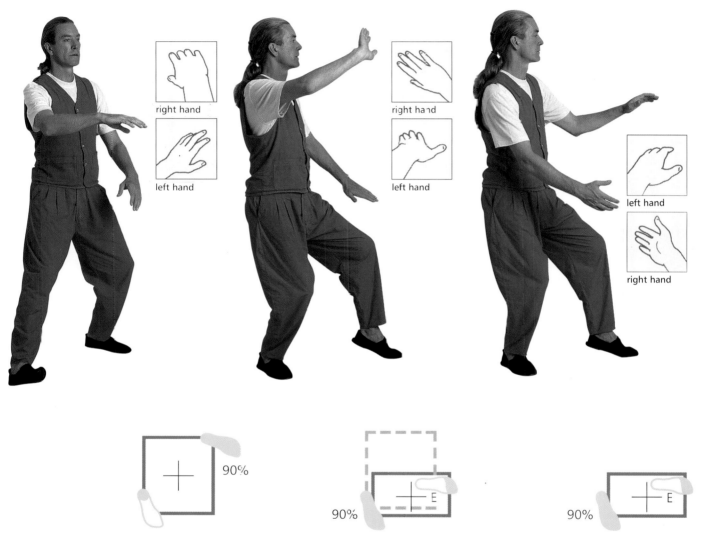

27 *Breathe In*
This movement is said to emulate the spreading and drying of a great bird's wings in the sunshine and is one of the most beautiful and elegant of all tai chi stances. Begin by pivoting a little on your right heel to help direct your center around to an east-facing position. This prepares you for a narrow toe stance toward the east.

27a *In-breath Finishes*
As you form a narrow toe stance with your left foot, your arms become like great wings – broad, powerful and expansive. The left hand drops to hover above the left thigh, while the right hand rises to make an extravagant kind of salute, almost as if you were shielding your eyes from the sun. Keep a little bit of energy in your left hand as well.

28 *Breathe Out*
Keeping your feet still, change the wings by lowering your right arm and raising the left. Your arms should move in curves rather than in straight lines up or down – rather like turning a giant steering wheel. Try to maintain the subtle energy connection between the palms as they pass each other and feel the buoyant energy of the crane in your limbs.

Brush Left Knee and Push

The term "brushing the knee" here is, of course, figurative. This movement, a natural continuation of the wide expansive movements of the crane's wings, enhances further our powers of balance and coordination and, in time, provides a wonderfully fluid, rotational quality to our movements.

right hand

right hand

left hand

90%

70%

E

E

front view

29 *Breathe In*
Begin to turn your waist clockwise and allow the right "wing" to circle back behind you – palm up at this stage, almost like holding an object in your right hand, ready to hurl. Meanwhile, your left hand has circled up and over toward your center in the process of making a small clockwise circle. Keep your head and shoulders properly aligned with your hips. Focus your eyes on your right palm as it drifts back.

30 *Breathe Out*
Step wide with your left foot, and as you do, "brush" across your left knee with your left palm, from right to left, turning your waist counterclockwise as you go. Keep your left hand at a good distance from your leg, say 8 in., throughout this movement, then, push out toward the east with your right hand. You finish in a wide 70/30 stance to the east – once again on those railroad tracks, your whole body facing east, left knee over left toes, and your eyes looking toward the distant horizon. Note the central position of the right palm at the end of this movement – not out to the south, but in line with the center of the chest.

Play Guitar (Left Side)

The following movement is similar to that found on page 33, only done on the other side, with the left foot leading. So we will now need to distinguish *between this Play Guitar and the one encountered previously, which was Play Guitar Right (right side leading); this is Play Guitar Left (left side leading).*

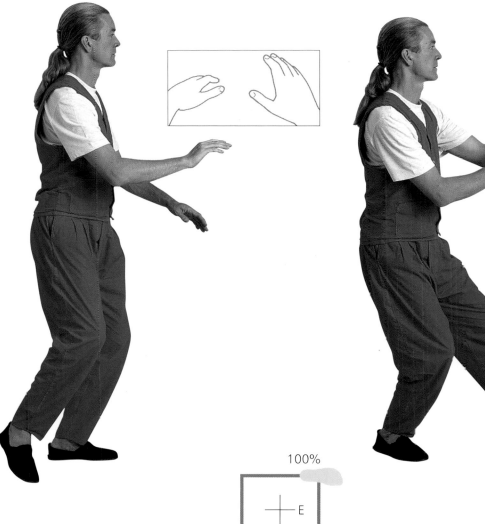

100%

90%

31 *Breathe In*
Transferring all your weight into your left foot for a moment, allow your back foot to leave the ground and follow through, just a short way, rather like kicking a soccer ball with the inside of the foot. This is really a little side-step to test your balance before returning your foot back down behind you again in roughly the same place as it was before. As this occurs, the hands relax, your wrists dropping a little with the in-breath.

32 *Breathe Out*
Sitting back into the rear leg, draw your left heel across and place it down in a narrow stance ahead of your right foot. As you do this, your hands close in on each other, this time with your left arm extended a little further than the right, with the palm of your right hand facing your left forearm. Try to visualize your left palm in particular becoming energized, though keep it relaxed at the same time. Your hips and shoulders should still be facing east.

Brush Left Knee and Push

This, again, is a repetition of a movement already learned (see page 36). The difference here is that you are approaching it from a narrow heel stance (as in Play Guitar), whereas previously it was approached from a narrow toe stance (as in Crane Spreads Its Wings).

right hand

right hand

left hand

70%

90%

33 *Breathe In*
Relax your hands, turn your waist clockwise and circle your right palm back behind you. As before *(see page 36)*, watch your palm go back from the corner of your eye, keeping your head squared up with your shoulders as your waist turns. You will find that it really does help to visualize a light, flat object in your palm, as if ready to hurl. This will help you to achieve the correct orientation of the right hand more easily.

34 *Breathe Out*
Return your center to the east once more by rotating your waist counterclockwise and step out, good and wide, with the left foot. Brush your left knee with your left palm as you go (remembering the distance between your palm and leg) and then push out east with your right palm as your left knee bends and your weight goes forward again. Your hips and shoulders face east at the finish. Your left hand should remain slightly energized at the end of this movement; do not let it "flop" or drop away behind you once you have completed the brush knee.

Step Forward, Parry and Punch

This sequence in particular reminds us of tai chi's martial origins. However, the fist here is not an angry fist, but rather a demonstration of our will and self-determination. It is also a particularly powerful means of concentrating mental energy and directing the chi.

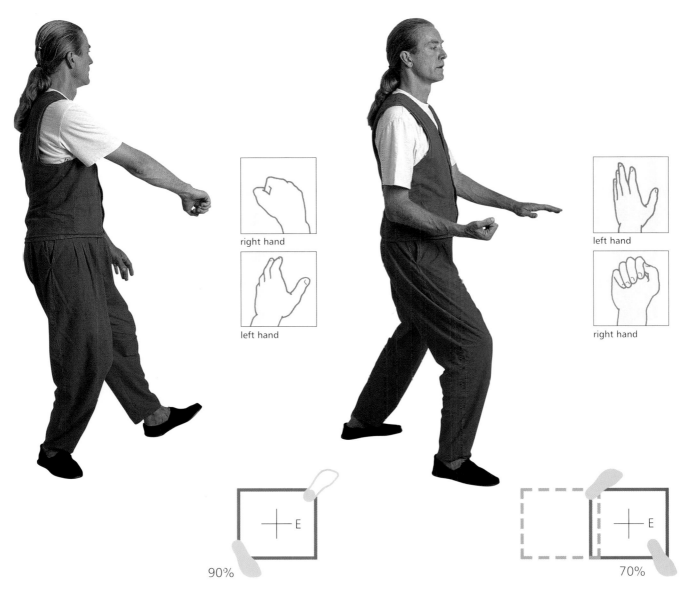

right hand

left hand

90%

left hand

right hand

70%

35 *Breathe In*
As we go through this sequence we are going to count the movements of the feet – one, two and three. This makes the learning process easier. Begin by forming a loose fist in your right hand – it should be rounded and clean in shape, though without tightness – then lower your arms to the left side and, shifting your weight momentarily from your left foot, turn out your left toes by pivoting on the heel. Put your foot down flat on the ground and mentally count out the number *one*.

36 *Breathe Out*
Step forward with your right foot and plant it down with the toes pointing out, roughly southeast, and mentally count out the number *two*. With this, "throw" the fist in a graceful arc across your center and around to your right hip, to finish with the knuckle side of the hand pointing downward. Your left palm follows to settle in the center, your arm almost horizontal at this stage. Then bring your weight over into your right side by bending your right knee.

Step Forward, Parry and Punch (continued)

When you come to the final punch, it should co-ordinate with the bending of the left knee to carry your weight forward at the same time. But do remember – the tai chi form is always done in a spirit of calmness and relaxation. Do not get excited by the idea of punching! Keep it slow.

left hand

left hand

right hand

70%

100%

37 *Breathe In*
With your weight now in your right side, lift your left foot from the ground and prepare to step forward toward the east by drawing in your toes just a little toward your right heel. Allow your waist to turn slightly in a clockwise direction and draw back the fist in your right hand, knuckles still facing downward, ready to punch. At the same time the left forearm starts to rise, ready to parry – that is, to deflect an oncoming force away to the left-hand side.

38 *Breathe Out*
Step straight ahead with your left foot and mentally count out the number *three*. This is your third and final step. As you do this, parry with the left forearm, sweeping out to the north from the center. Then, as your left knee bends and your weight goes forward, punch to the east very slowly, in the center, about solar-plexus height. As your fist goes forward it does a half-turn in midflight to finish with the thumb side uppermost. Adjust your back heel to a comfortable position if necessary.

Release Arm and Push

This is an excellent exercise for aiding relaxation in the wrist and elbow joints. Anatomically speaking, remember that whenever we rotate our wrists, the movement comes from the elbows. You will also find *that there is a fair amount of activity in the wrists, too, as they rotate outward and inward during the course of the movement. Keep some space between your elbows and your sides.*

70%

70%

70%

39 *Breathe In*
With your right arm still extended, turn your waist a little to the left and slide your left hand, palm down, beneath your right forearm. Now let go of the fist in your right hand and turn both palms up. As you do this, reverse the turn in your waist, draw your right hand back across your left forearm and sit back into the rear leg. Allow your left hand to follow the right, close to your center.

39a *In-breath Finishes*
At the end of the inhalation the hands are in the process of rotating into a palms-out position, ready to push forward, the waist has turned slightly clockwise and the weight has transferred into the back leg. Again, maintain an open aspect to the arms, with lots of space between your elbows and body. Keep your spine straight, without leaning backward, and do not lock the front knee.

40 *Breathe Out*
Bend your left knee and bring your weight slowly forward again as you push out to the east with your palms at about chest height. Your thumbs should be pointing toward each other and your hands roughly covering the center of your chest. This is very similar to the push shown on page 29, only here the left foot is forward. As with all the pushes, make sure you are not tempted to lean.

Turn and Cross Hands

Traditionally, this movement is placed at the end of what is called the "first part" of the short yang form. It has a flourish and a distinct character of closing up and of sealing the energies, and we will meet with it again at the conclusion of the whole form later on in this book.

41 *Breathe In*
Transferring most of your weight once again into the rear leg, relax your hands and lift your left toes, keeping your heel on the ground. Your hands should look like you are warming them at a fire. Prepare to pivot on your left heel to turn your waist toward the south; most of your weight remains in the right foot, with your gaze directed inward. Keep those shoulders relaxed!

42 *Breathe Out*
Having turned your left foot to point as near south as you can, bring the weight back into your left side and begin to draw your right foot back, with the toes pointing south and making only the lightest of contact with the ground. Meanwhile, as you turn your body toward the south, your hands start to separate out in what will shortly become two halves of a great circle which you will "draw" in the air.

42a *Out-breath Finishes*
The turn concludes with the hands having descended in two sweeping arcs to complete a circle at the level of the abdomen. The feet should now be alongside each other in a parallel, shoulder-width stance. Also, your palms should face slightly inward, just as the out-breath finishes, with your elbows well-spaced away from your sides as though embracing a great sphere. Let your weight sink down.

42

Turn and Cross Hands (continued)

The idea portrayed here is of enclosing the energies and returning them, even if only momentarily, back to the Tan Tien – the vital center in the abdomen.

Try and cultivate that feeling, as it really does help to bring about genuine changes in the inner physiology of the body.

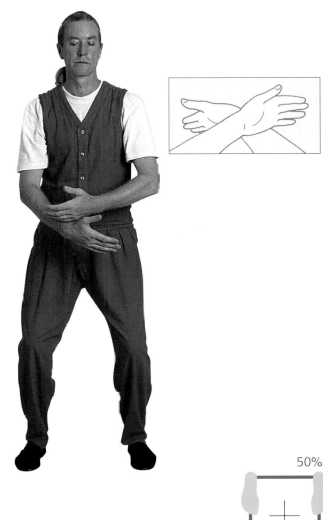

50%

50%

43 *Breathe In*
With your feet now parallel and the toes pointing south, and having completed the circle with your hands at the level of the abdomen, lift your hands up through the center of the body to cross (left wrist on top of right) at about chin height. In other words, the left forearm is closer to you than the right as the wrists cross. Keep your shoulders relaxed as you raise your arms and do not tighten your knees. Keep the whole of your body straight, perfectly aligned and calm.

44 *Breathe Out*
Lower both hands down through your center and let your weight sink down. As mentioned earlier, this is a traditional closing movement, and it is always possible to finish your tai chi session at this point. Here, however, we are going to prepare for the next movements of the form by bringing a good percentage of our weight into the left side, with the back of the left hand trailing along the right forearm as the hands go down.

FOUR
Finding the Diagonal

Here we step for the first time onto the diagonal axis. Movements of this kind present a fresh challenge, helping us to develop our own sense of orientation. We are now compelled to work in relation to our own center, without reference to our surroundings – the walls of the room, for example, are no longer of use in lining things up. This enhanced self-awareness is an important stage in the tai chi journey.

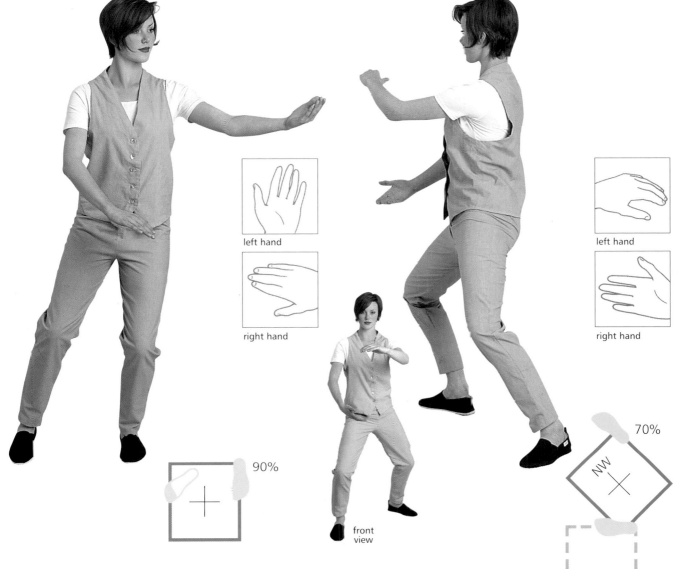

Carry the Tiger to the Mountain

In the ancient classic, the I Ching *or* Book of Changes *(c. 1100 B.C.), nine directions are mentioned: the cardinal points, the four points in between and the all-important center, each one symbolic of a natural* environmental force. The northwest is the direction of the mountain, of stillness and repose. The tiger is equated with the "life force," so here you are transferring your vital force toward the northwest.*

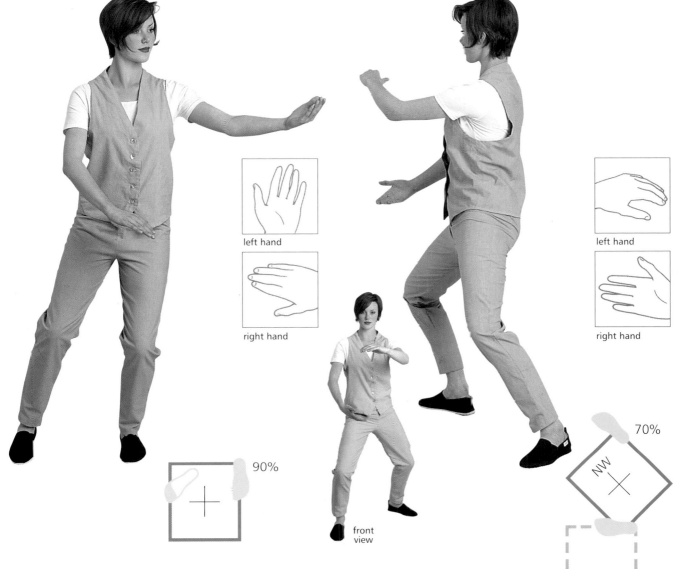

left hand

right hand

left hand

right hand

90%

70%

NW

front view

45 *Breathe In*
From Turn and Cross Hands at the end of the last section, having uncrossed your hands to your left now raise your right heel and transfer your weight into your left side. With your hips and shoulders facing southeast, your left palm rises to about chest height. Then prepare to step around to the northwest by drawing your right toes in a little closer toward your left heel. This is a big step coming up, so make certain you feel properly balanced in your left side before commiting yourself to the turn.

46 *Breathe Out*
Rotate your waist clockwise and step around to set your right foot down, heel first, pointing northwest. As you go, your right palm "brushes" your right thigh, then turns upward as your right knee bends and the weight settles in your right side. Your left hand, meanwhile, comes across, palm facing down now, to form a ball at your right side with your right hand underneath. To avoid any undue strain on the left knee, adjust your back foot to a comfortable position as soon as the weight settles in your right side. Your hips and shoulders should remain aligned throughout the movement.

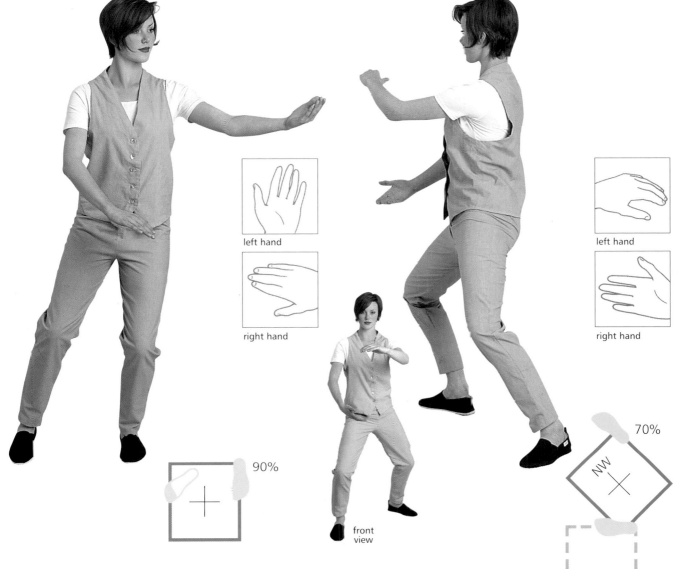

Diagonal Rollback and Press

Nowhere is the relationship between the hands and waist so clearly illustrated as in this sequence; it is, in fact, the waist that creates much of the movement. We are now in the process of repeating a whole string of movements taken from Section Two.

This is the second rendition of the Chorus (see pages 27–31) which occurs four times in all, and Grasp the Bird's Tail is not repeated here as Carry the Tiger has taken its place. The action remains on the diagonal axis: northwest to southeast.

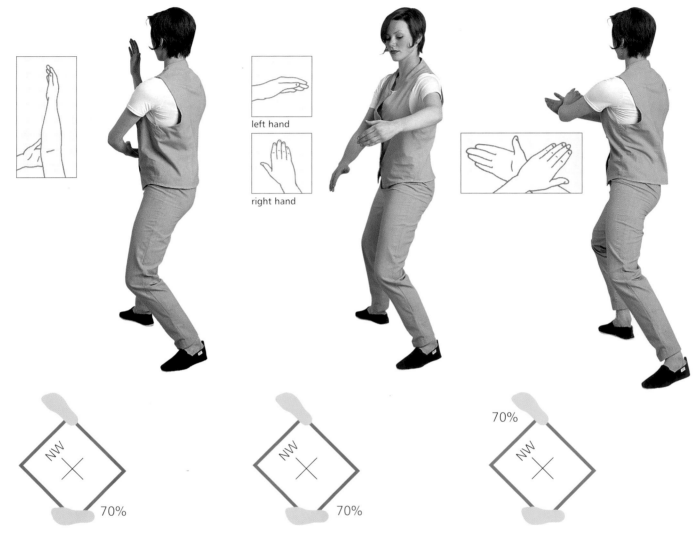

47 *Breathe In*
With your head, hips and shoulders all facing northwest, sit back into the rear leg and move your arms, raising the right and dropping the left by "sliding" it along the right forearm to cup the right elbow. This is the Rollback position, exactly the same as on page 28, only this time it is done toward the "mountain"; the waist turns slightly to the right. Do not lock the front knee as you sit back.

47a *In-breath Finishes*
Turn your waist counterclockwise and circle your left hand back, while folding over your right forearm across your center. Newcomers to tai chi often perceive this movement as complex and difficult to learn; just relax and let your arms find their places naturally as your waist turns and your knees bend. There should be a little more weight in your back leg than in the previous stance.

48 *Breathe Out*
Rotate and turn your palms to face each other and then bend your right knee, turning your waist back toward the northwest. As you do this, allow your left palm to approach your right until the heels of the palms make contact very lightly in front of your chest. Most of the hand energy is now concentrated in your left hand, to mirror the substantial right leg. Hips and shoulders face northwest.

Diagonal Push

The push here is identical to the push as illustrated in Section Two (see page 29), but is shown again from this angle to illustrate the width of the stance – *all based on the 70/30 ratio, of course, with the weight shifting back and forth. Notice how both knees remain soft, never locked.*

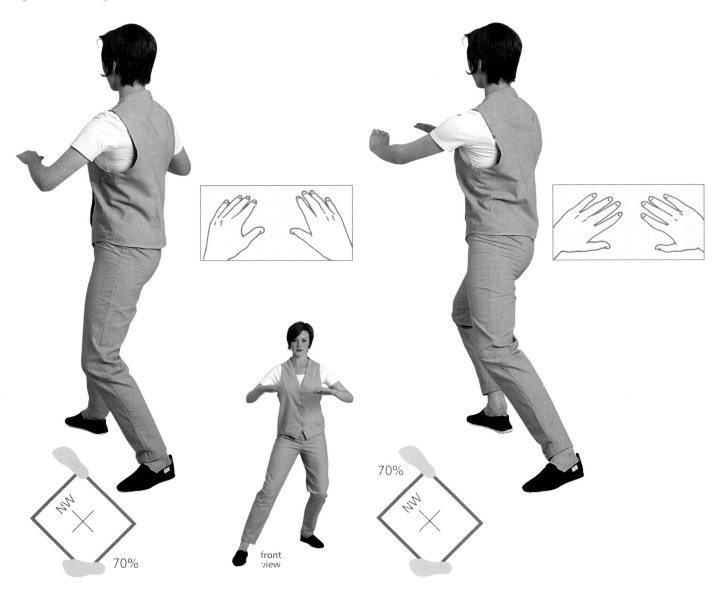

70%

70%

front view

49 *Breathe In*
As before, with hips and shoulders facing northwest, separate your hands and then sit back once more into the rear leg. It is worth noting here (and in fact, this applies every time you do this movement) that as you separate your hands from the press, try to do so by trailing your right thumb across your left palm. This ensures a rolling and "sliding-apart" appearance to the hands which is particularly smooth and pleasing.

50 *Breathe Out*
Slowly rotate your palms to face ahead without creating a sharp angle at the wrist joint and then, shifting your weight forward once again, push toward the northwest at about chest height. Your hips and shoulders should also be facing northwest. Make sure that your hands are relatively central and not spread out wide to the sides. Your thumbs should be about 10 in. apart at the most, although this will depend on your overall size. You might also like to cultivate a slight "lifting" movement to the push, with your hands rising upward a little as they go forward.

Diagonal Single Whip

Continual use of the diagonals helps us to under-stand our relationship with our vital center. The challenge here is to execute the turn to the southeast and yet still maintain the correct width between the feet. The "railroad tracks" are still there, only run-ning diagonally.

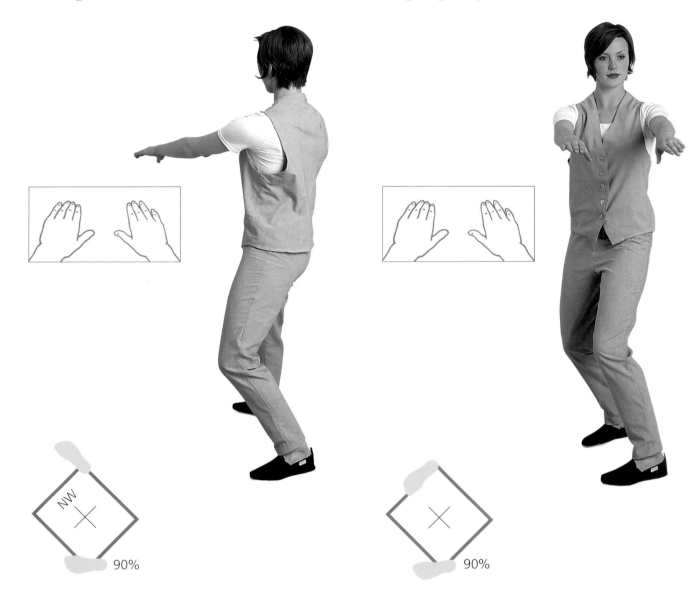

51 *Breathe In*
From your northwest facing position, sit back into the rear leg and allow your arms to straighten, your palms facing downward. This time, the Single Whip is a real test of your spatial coordination by going from northwest to finish facing southeast. In every other respect, however, it is exactly the same movement as shown on pages 30–31. (Note: you can also find this movement – and, indeed, the whole of the Chorus – illustrated in small scale on page 87.)

52 *Breathe Out*
With your weight mostly in the left side, pivot very slowly on your right heel to turn your waist counterclockwise, allowing your arms to follow your center as your waist turns and your feet take on the slightly pigeon-toed stance typical of this stage of the Single Whip. Remember to let your waist turn freely about its axis (the spine) and to shift your weight clearly back and forth between your left and right legs as the turning takes place. Even though your arms are relatively straight, do not lock your elbows at any time.

Diagonal Single Whip (continued)

The turning of the waist, both to the left and to the right, is clearly shown if you compare this view of the Single Whip with that shown on pages 30–31.

Do not despair if it takes a while to build up flexibility in this area. Learn the movements thoroughly first, and gradually the flexibility will appear.

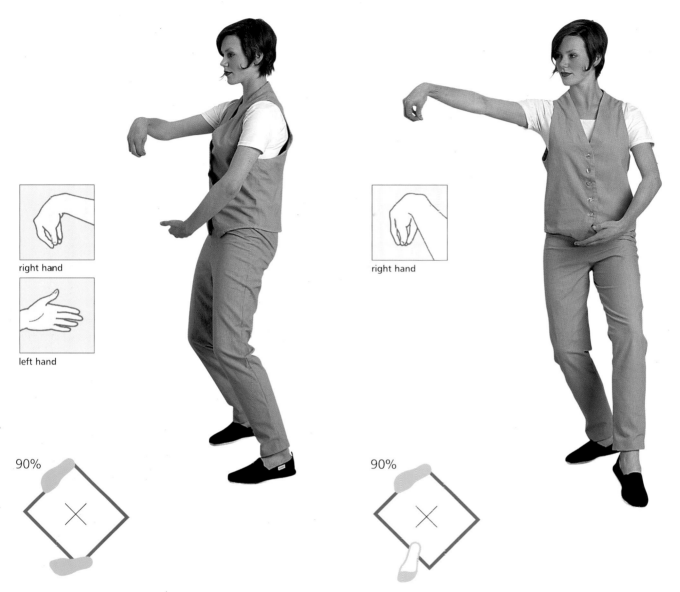

right hand

left hand

90%

right hand

90%

53 *Breathe In*
Now the waist reverses direction once more, rotating clockwise, while the right hand is drawn back horizontally in front of your right shoulder to form the crane's beak in the hand – the wrist loose, the fingers pointing downward and the index finger and thumb lightly touching, like holding a pinch of salt. Your left hand, meanwhile, swoops down, palm facing upward, to settle near your right hip. You can think of this movement as a "scooping-up" motion, as though you were scooping up sand using the palm of your left hand.

54 *Breathe Out*
With most of your weight now in the right side, pivot on your left toes by raising your left heel. Your waist turns counterclockwise once again as you straighten your right arm to project your crane's beak toward the west, keeping your gaze directed roughly in the region of your right hand as it goes. Make sure you keep your elbow soft and relaxed. Certainly, the arm appears to be nearly straight, but it is not – not quite. Always keep a little in reserve.

Diagonal Single Whip (continued)

As you step around at the conclusion of this move-ment, it is important to keep the width between your feet. As the "railroad tracks" here run from northwest *to southeast, you need to swing your left hip around good and wide to establish the correct stance. This is the last movement of the Chorus.*

left hand

100%

left hand

SE

70%

55 *Breathe In*
For the final stages of the Single Whip, empty all the weight from your left side and prepare to step around to the southeast by drawing your left toes in a little toward your right heel. Your left hand rises at this point, palm facing in; it is useful to continue with the metaphor of the sand here – that is, having scooped up the sand with your left palm, allow the sand to trickle from your fingers as you turn your palm inward and lift it. Keep your gaze directed on your left palm for a moment.

56 *Breathe Out*
Rotate your waist, step around to the south-east with your left heel and bend your knee. As soon as the weight returns to your left side, adjust the back foot to a comfortable position by pivoting on your right heel to get your hips and shoulders facing south-east. Your left hand rotates to point outward, as if toward the distant horizon, and your right arm, still extended and still with its crane's beak intact, is slight-ly behind you, remaining as a focus of concentration. The left shoulder stays relaxed, but do not let your arm go weak.

Fist Under Elbow

Here we return to the east–west axis, using another one-two-three step. Again, as with Step Forward, Parry and Punch, while you are learning this movement it is a good idea to count the steps as you go, either aloud or mentally to yourself. Another fist is featured here, but again it is a relaxed and loose fist. Some people describe it as like holding an egg or even a small bird. It should be that delicate – no pressure. Also, the fist is not directly under the elbow, but rather just to the inside of it.

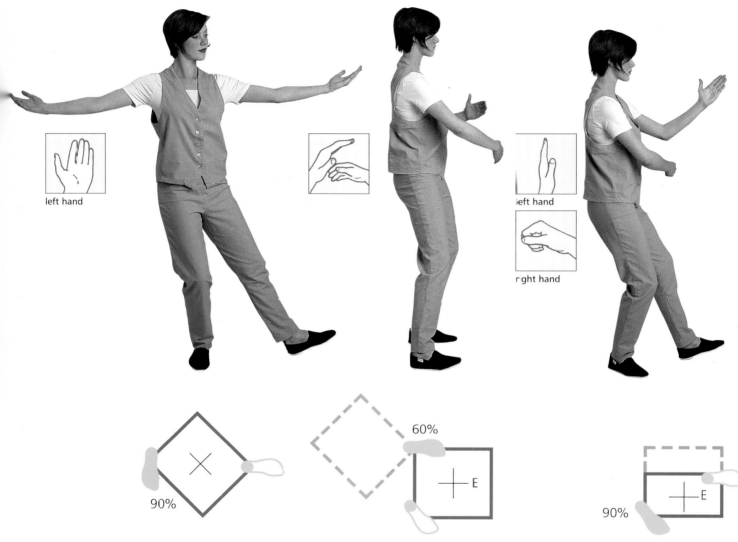

left hand

left hand

right hand

90%

60%

E

90%

E

57 *Breathe In*
Shift the weight from your left foot and sit back on your rear leg. Let go of the crane's beak, relax your elbows and open your hands, palms up, one at a time (first the right, and then the left). Next, pivot on your left heel to point the toes due east and then set your foot down flat on the ground, bending your left knee to bring the weight forward once again. That's step number *one*.

57a *In-breath Finishes*
Draw up your right foot and place it alongside the left with the toes pointing out (step number *two*). Then bring your weight forward into your right side, allowing your waist to turn naturally to get your hips and shoulders facing east just as your in-breath is finishing. Meanwhile, your arms drop around and down, slightly to your left, with your palms still open, your left hand slightly higher than your right.

58 *Breathe Out*
With your weight now in your right side, slide your left foot forward into a narrow heel stance to the east (step number *three*). At the same time drop your right arm a little lower and project your left hand and forearm forward and across to point the fingers due east at chin height. The left hand should be flat, while the right hand forms a fist which comes to rest just inside, to the south of the left elbow.

51

FIVE

Stepping Back and Stepping Sideways

Some radical changes in the character of stepping occur in this
section. The focus here is on the rear and the sides of the body and on motion
in these directions. Both these developments engender a further increase in our
powers of coordination and spatial awareness and feature sequences of
wonderfully rhythmic, flowing movement.

Repulse Monkey, Right Side

The monkey is a deity in oriental culture, playful and mischievous, but also wise. The broad, swinging movements of the limbs here mimic those of the monkey, being light and graceful. This is a fascinating movement which is repeated three times in succession, on alternate sides.

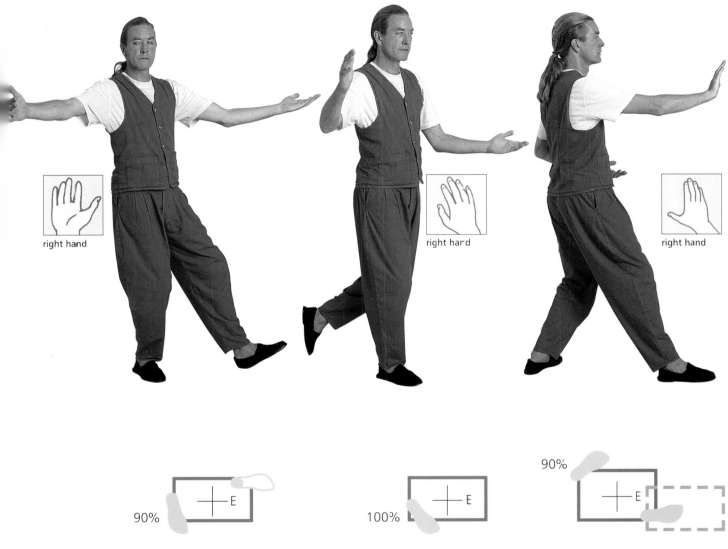

59 *Breathe In*
Still in the narrow heel stance from Fist Under Elbow *(see left)*, let go of the fist in your right hand and turn up your left palm. You can think of this as offering the monkey some food, tempting him to come down from the trees. Then turn your waist clockwise and circle your right palm back behind you, watching your hand out of the corner of your eye. Meanwhile sink your weight into your right side.

60 *Breathe Out*
Having raised your left foot from the ground by sinking into your right side at the end of the in-breath, now step back behind with your left foot, making contact with the toes first. As you step back, begin to lower your left hand to your side by bringing your elbow down and drawing it back. Your right arm begins to move around to the front in preparation for the push in the next step.

60a *Out-breath Finishes*
Now shift all of your weight back into your left foot, and push out toward the east with your right palm. You can think of this as pushing the monkey's nose, just as he comes to get the food that you were holding in your left hand. At the end of the movement, as you push forward, adjust the front foot to turn the toes east. That is the end of the first Repulse Monkey.

Repulse Monkey, Left Side

There is always a danger of stepping back too narrow with the Repulse Monkey sequence and losing your balance in the process. Although most of your weight goes into the rear leg each time, the stance should still be fairly wide. Try thinking of stepping back diagonally rather than straight behind you.

left hand

left hand

100%

90%

61 *Breathe In*
For the second Repulse Monkey we are going to repeat the previous movement, only on the other side. So begin by turning up your right palm this time and circling back with your left hand as your waist turns counterclockwise. Do not turn your waist until you have turned up your right palm. In tai chi we try to distinguish between the various elements of any movement, rather than doing them all at once, as this would only dissipate the energy into too many places at the same time.

62 *Breathe Out*
Step back with your right foot this time, making contact with your toes first while lowering your right hand to your side. Then shift all of your weight back into your right foot and push out east with your left palm. Here, again, you are pushing the monkey's nose just as he comes to take the offering. And again, at the end of the movement, as you push forward, adjust the front foot to turn the toes east. That is the end of the second Repulse Monkey. Keep the front foot flat on the ground once you have adjusted it.

Repulse Monkey, Right Side

With Repulse Monkey, Master Cheng advocated step-ping back with the feet parallel to each other, which has a stimulating effect on the area at the base of the spine. This is not easy for beginners, however, and so here we use a slightly older version of the steps, as found in the traditional long form.

right hand

right hand

90%

90%

63 *Breathe In*
Repulse Monkey number three is much the same as number one, except that we are now coming to it from a position where the left foot is already flat on the ground instead of in a left heel stance (Fist Under Elbow). Otherwise it is the same. So, as before, turn up your left palm and then turn your waist to the south and lift your right palm back behind you. The shape of the palm in all these Repulse Monkey movements is, once again, rather like holding a flat object, ready to hurl, but keep the arm and hand relaxed.

64 *Breathe Out*
Step back behind with your left foot, again making contact with the toes first. Simultaneously lower your left hand to your side, shift your weight back into your left foot and push out east with your right palm. At the end of the movement, adjust your front foot to turn the toes east. Your left arm, as it descends, should do so with plenty of space between the elbow and your body – looking for a moment rather like you are carrying a rolled blanket tucked under your arm. This also applies to Repulse Monkey on the other side.

Diagonal Flying

This movement sometimes also goes by the name of Slant Flying. Again we meet with another large three-quarter turn, and a very expansive one, the *arms separating out in wide graceful sweeps as you go. You may find it helpful to think of a spring being coiled inward and then spiraling out again.*

left hand

right hand

right hand

90%

front view

70%

SW

65 *Breathe In*
Keeping for a moment with the image of the monkey, here we are going to respectfully finish our game and simply pick up the monkey and help it back into the tree. Pivot on your right heel and turn your waist counterclockwise as you drop your right hand around to your left hip, bringing your left hand up and around to help form a ball toward the northeast, left hand on top, right hand underneath. Then with all your weight in your left side, draw your right toes in a little toward your left heel in preparation for the next step.

66 *Breathe Out*
Having "picked up" the monkey, turn your waist clockwise and step right around to put your right foot down, heel first, toward the southwest. Do not forget to adjust your back foot to a comfortable position as soon as possible, and as you turn, change your hands by raising your right arm in a great arc up toward the southwest, palm facing in, while the left hand, still with plenty of energy remaining in it, drops back down to about hip height. Your right arm should rise to the outside of your left arm – putting the monkey back in the tree.

Wave Hands Like Clouds (Transitional Phase)

We transfer here into another lengthy sequence in which movements are repeated on alternate sides, this time featuring sideways stepping. But before *this sequence begins, however, there is an important transitional movement to bring us once again back onto the east–west axis.*

right hand

left hand

90%

left hand

right hand

70%

S

67 *Breathe In*
Bring your left foot up alongside your right foot at a distance of at least one-and-a-half shoulder widths. Make contact with your heel first as you step and set your foot down with the toes pointing south. At the same time swoop around with your left hand, palm down initially but changing to an inward-facing position as it goes, and bring it to settle beneath your right hand, which has also rotated slightly to turn palm down, thereby forming an approximate ball between your hands.

68 *Breathe Out*
Begin to shift your weight from your right foot back across into your left side and, as the weight changes, rotate your left palm a little to complete the ball (which does not need to be too well defined in this instance). Then change hands – that is, lower your right hand down to about hip height and raise your left to about throat height. The upper arm extends along slightly to make room for the lower one to rise. Most of your weight has now gone into your left side, and your hips and shoulders should be facing south.

Wave Hands Like Clouds, Left Side

The movements are shown here in detail, with two photographs to cover the in-breath (yin) phase of each one. Please note, however, that the speed of *your breathing should not alter; in other words, the length of inhalation should not become longer just because there are two photographs to show it.*

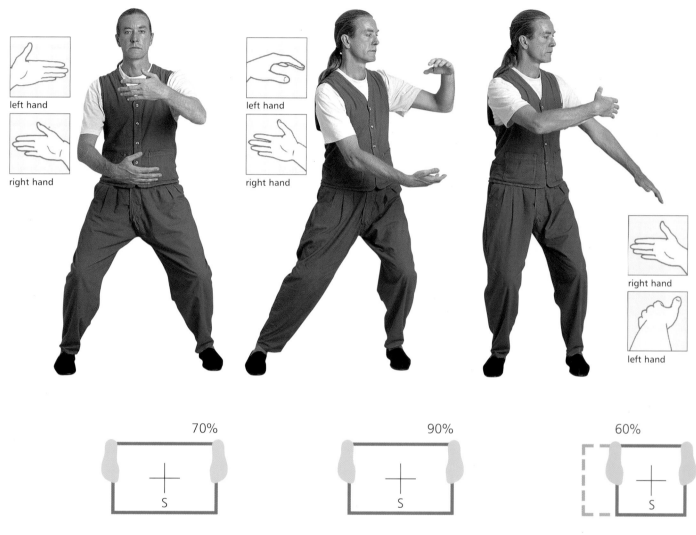

left hand

right hand

left hand

right hand

right hand

left hand

70%

90%

60%

69 *Breathe In* Tuck your right toes in to point south, parallel with your left foot, and position your hands one above the other, your left palm facing your throat, your right palm facing your navel. Your in-breath begins here, as you finish squaring up. Your hands should be a good distance away from your body — about 12 in., depending on your own proportions and height. Keep the knees apart, "spiraled" out.

69a *In-breath Finishes* Slowly turn your waist counterclockwise and, again slowly, rotate your wrists to form a ball, left hand on top. Not too far with the turning of the waist! Never turn to such an extent that you introduce tension; your knees should not cave in toward each other with the turn; your waist should not feel tight; and your buttocks should not stick out. You complete the in-breath with this turn.

70 *Breathe Out* With most of your weight now settled in your left side, step inward with your right foot, so that it is shoulder width from your left and parallel, toes pointing south. Then as the weight settles slightly more in your right side, change your hands by lowering the left and raising the right. The upper arm extends slightly along, in this case to the east, to make space for the lower one to rise to the inside of it.

Wave Hands Like Clouds, Right Side

With the steps in Wave Hands Like Clouds (sometimes simply called Cloudy Hands) try to keep your feet parallel to each other at all times. It is almost a kind of "plodding" motion as you step sideways, the knees apart, the center of gravity low. With this sequence turning your waist without tension is absolutely vital. Direct your breathing into your abdomen and visualize your whole spinal column rotating while keeping your head and shoulders squared up as you go.

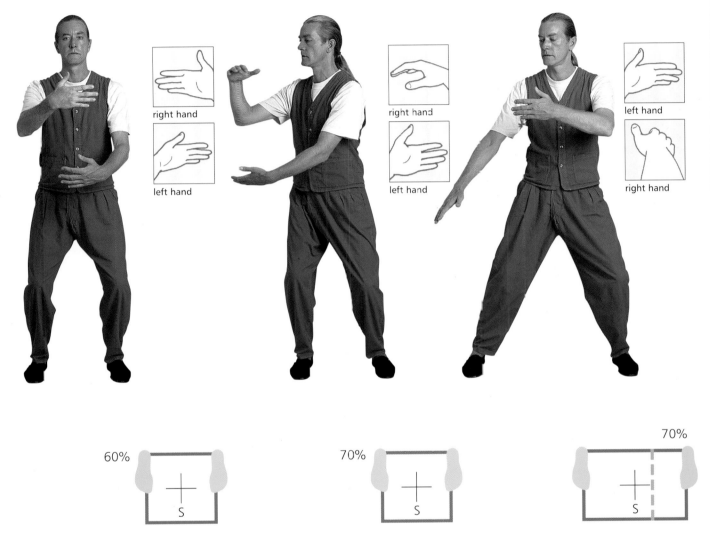

71 *Breathe In*
You are now going to repeat what you have just learned, but on the other side. Begin by turning your waist back to your south-facing position, continuing to shift your weight into your right leg as you go. This time, the right palm is positioned facing the throat with the left palm below, facing the navel. Do not linger in this position; treat it as part of the wider turn to the right, which comes next.

71a *In-breath Finishes*
Turning your waist clockwise this time, form another ball with your hands, right hand on top. Do not exaggerate the ball shape; in tai chi "holding a ball" means that an energy connection should exist between the palms. As long as you have that feeling, if only on an imaginative level at first, it is enough. You do not need to spell it out by creating a precise shape, as if holding an actual ball.

72 *Breathe Out*
With most of your weight now in your right side, step further out toward the east with your left foot, toes still pointing south, so that there is at least one-and-a-half shoulder widths between your feet. Then, as the weight settles in your left side, change hands by lowering the right and raising the left. Again, the upper arm extends slightly to the west to make space for the lower one to rise to the inside of it.

59

Wave Hands Like Clouds, Left Side

We are now going to repeat this movement to the left, and we could, if we wished, continue in this way indefinitely, stepping from west to east – but we do not. In the short yang form, this is usually the final

Wave Hands in the sequence. Here, we conclude by stepping forward into the final stages of a Single Whip. This is the only time it occurs on its own in the whole of the form without being part of the Chorus.

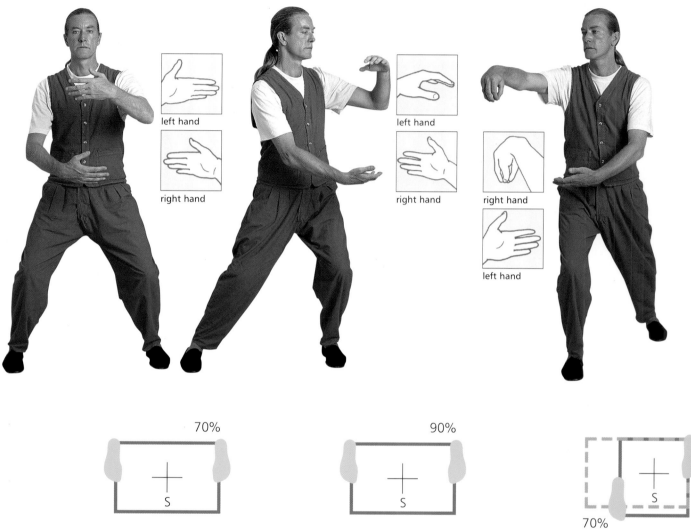

73 *Breathe In*
Turn back to your south-facing position – keeping your feet in the same place – with your left palm facing your throat and your right palm facing your navel. It is tempting to ignore this "squaring up" stage and simply go straight around, turning from one side to the other. However, you should always return to this south-facing position to get your bearings before continuing around to the side.

73a *In-breath Finishes*
Turn your waist counterclockwise and form a ball with your hands, left hand on top, palm down. Always rotate your wrists slowly as you form the ball, keeping your hands relaxed throughout. Be precise about this. As part of the learning process, it is sometimes necessary to adopt a methodical approach at first; be patient, concentrate, and you will soon "free up" more during this movement.

74 *Breathe Out*
This time, step forward a half-pace with your right foot, heel first, and shift your weight forward by bending your knee. Move your foot in as you step, so that your feet are shoulder-width apart. Then, as your hands change, your right hand rises in the form of a crane's beak and your left palm turns upward, following around to settle beneath, near your right hip; your waist can turn a little clockwise as you go.

Single Whip

As you complete the Single Whip here, remember not to let go of the crane's beak in your right hand or allow it to droop or become weak. It remains intact throughout, the arm almost straight, a continued focus of attention. Try to make the final step a long one, ready for the next move.

left hand

left hand

100%

70%

front view

75 *Breathe In*
Prepare to finish off the Single Whip now by emptying the weight from your left foot and drawing your left toes in a little closer to your right heel, ready to step east. Continue to sink your weight into your right side as your left palm begins to rise, thereby altering from a palm-up position to one in which the palm is facing inward. As with previous closing stages of the Single Whip, you might find it helpful to focus your eyes on your palm to ensure the correct orientation of your arm.

76 *Breathe Out*
Step around slowly to the east with your left foot, heel first, good and wide, and bend your knee. As soon as the weight returns to your left side, adjust the back foot to a comfortable position by pivoting on your right heel to get your hips and shoulders facing east. As before, at the end of the Single Whip the left hand rotates to point the fingertips outward, as if toward a distant horizon, the elbow rounded and soft. Your left hand should be in line with the left side of your chest – do not let it drift out to the side. The energy of the crane's beak in your right hand balances the substantial energy contained in your left leg.

61

SIX

Downward and Upward

In tai chi we usually try to keep a smooth, level appearance to our movements. However, in this section things are a little different. Here, we not only dip and rise deliberately, but we also meet with stances in which one foot leaves the ground in order to kick, all of which really gets to work on those leg muscles. The focus is on keeping the "root," the sense of being connected firmly to the energies of the earth.

Snake Creeps Down

This is also sometimes called the Squatting Single Whip, on account of the crane's beak that remains in the right hand. It is a very elegant, classical tai

chi movement often celebrated in painting and sculpture – although for those in the West it is also one of the most difficult to perform correctly.

left hand

left hand

90%

90%

77 *Breathe In*
From the Single Whip position at the finish of the last section, prepare for the next movement by first lengthening your stance by sliding or shuffling back (depending on the type of surface on which you are standing) with your right foot. The foot also turns as it goes back to point southwest. Then bring your weight into the rear leg and draw your left hand back a little toward your chest to face roughly southwest. Keep the crane's beak intact in your right hand.

77a *In-breath Finishes*
Now sit back into your right leg, lowering your body into a kind of squatting position while turning a little on your left heel to point the toes of the left foot inward, roughly southeast. At the same time continue to draw your left hand back toward your chest, flattened and blade-like, the palm now facing inward. Keep squatting as low as you can without discomfort. Do try to keep your body upright; in other words, do not lean forward just to get down a few inches lower.

Snake Creeps Down (continued)

Chang San-feng, the legendary founder of the original tai chi form, was inspired by a recurring dream in which a snake and a crane vied for a morsel of food. As the crane struck out with its beak, the snake *would recoil; as the snake darted back, the crane would enfold it and throw it using its wings. Neither creature was ever victorious, symbolizing a perfect balance between the two great forces of yin and yang.*

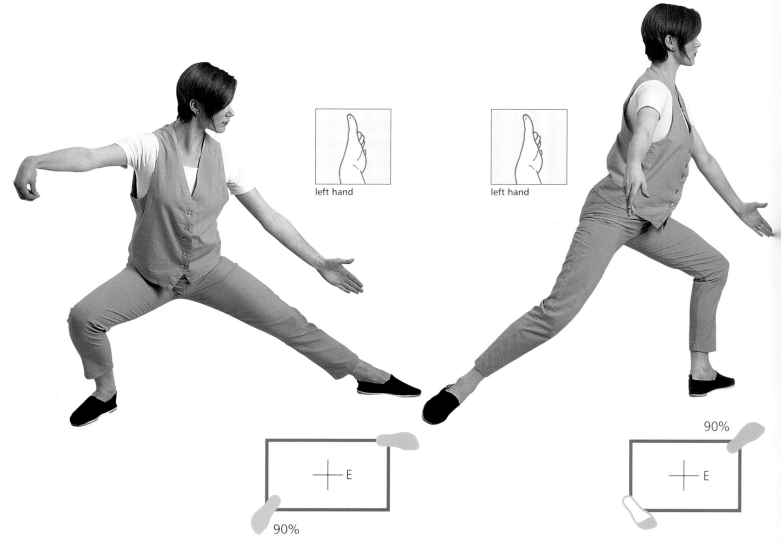

left hand

left hand

90%

90%

78 *Breathe Out*

Still squatting down with your weight mostly in the rear leg, allow your left hand to continue on its circular sweep downward and forward, close to the ground, the fingers leading and the palm, therefore, facing south. Your hand moves on past your foot and, as it goes, your foot straightens to point east once again. Note that there is still a slight bend to the left knee, even though the leg itself is almost straight. Above all, relax. Be comfortable! And never view your tai chi as some kind of stretching exercise; that can be done in the warm-up *(see pages 11–12).*

78a *Out-breath Finishes*

Raise your body a little and bring your weight forward, letting go of the crane's beak in your right hand. This releases the weight from your right foot and enables you to turn it inward again, pointing toward the southeast. As soon as this is accomplished, shift your weight backward and turn your left toes out by pivoting on your heel (your left foot is the back foot in the next stance, so you need to turn it out now). Finally bring your weight forward once more over your left foot. As you do this, your right heel comes up so that only your toes are touching the ground. You are now ready to go into Golden Pheasant.

Golden Pheasant Stands on Left Leg

This is very much a contrast to the previous movement. Whereas Snake Creeps Down was low and rather mysterious, here the Golden Pheasant is tall and very much "up-front." This is the male bird showing off, raising his wing and leg together. This is an unusual routine insofar as the most obvious part of the movement is accomplished on the inbreath rather than the out-breath.

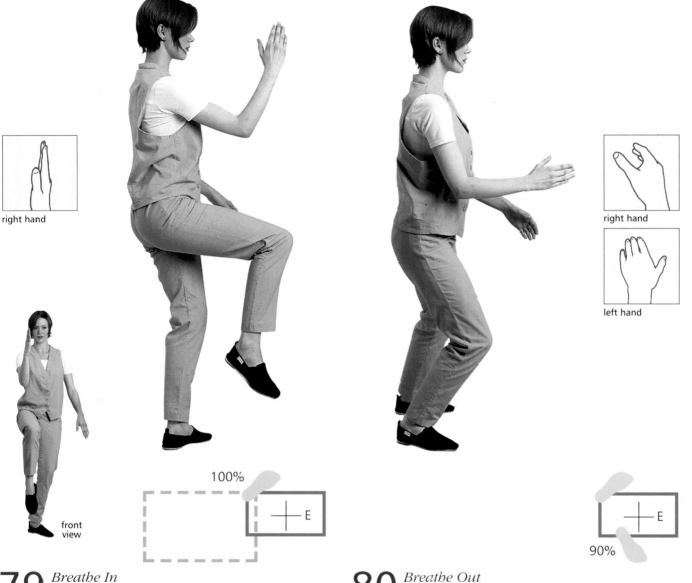

right hand

front view

right hand

left hand

100%

E

90%

E

79 *Breathe In*
Begin by making sure your left knee is over your left foot, then come forward and up, raising your right knee as far as is comfortable while almost simultaneously bringing up your right forearm, too, so that your elbow settles close above your right knee. In fact, the forearm, elbow, knee and shin should all be roughly aligned when seen from the front, and not sticking out to one side or the other. Your right palm should be facing north, while your left hand is relaxed by your side, palm facing down.

80 *Breathe Out*
Slowly lower your right arm and leg, making sure that as your right foot touches the ground it does so alongside the left about shoulder-width apart and with the toes pointing outward, roughly southeast. Allow your weight to settle in your right side and relax your right hand, with your fingers pointing slightly inward, and your palm now facing the ground. Sink well into your right foot and prepare to raise your left leg in just a moment in order to repeat the movement on the other side.

Golden Pheasant Stands on Right Leg

This is an excellent load-bearing exercise that also cultivates balance and poise. Concentrate on a smooth and gradual transition of energy from side to side as you change from your left leg to your right.

Pat the Horse on the Right

The horse is one of the most powerful of creatures, and yet its movements are always graceful and fluent. Here, the arms tend to resemble the way a horse's front legs roll and strike out when raised in the air.

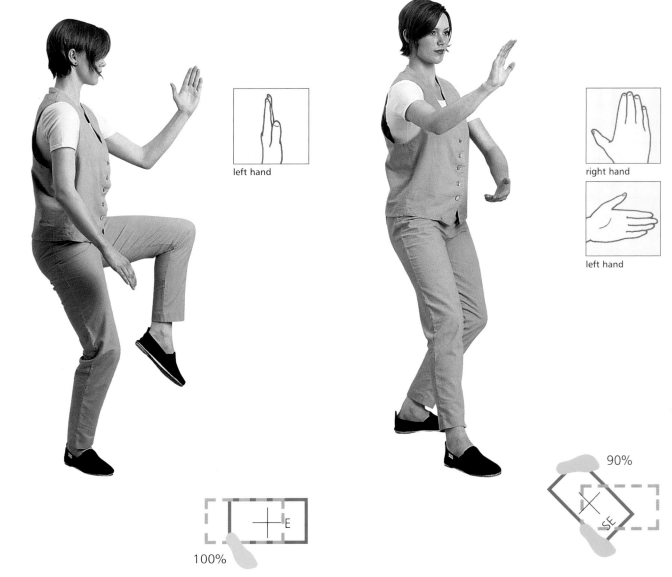

left hand

right hand

left hand

100%

90%

81 *Breathe In*
We are now going to repeat the previous movement on the opposite side. Once your weight is settled in your right side, slowly raise your left knee to a comfortable height along with your left arm. If your balance is really poor, keep the tips of your toes on the ground; it is important with these stances to feel calm and relaxed and to keep the back straight. Avoid scrunching up or leaning over as you rise into position. If you suspect that this is happening and your stomach feels tense, then simply lower your knee. Your right hand should be relaxed by your side, palm facing down.

82 *Breathe Out*
With your next out-breath lower your left arm and set your left foot down slightly to the rear, making contact with the toes first. Then, as the weight settles back into your left leg, slide your right palm forward, as if resting on the flank of a horse or pony. Your left hand, meanwhile, rotates to turn palm-up, as if holding an apple for the horse to eat. Keep your right hand relaxed, but note that as your weight goes into the rear leg, your right palm flattens out somewhat and becomes more energized. Do not worry if this movement does not come together right away – let it happen naturally.

66

Separate Hands and Kick With Right Toes

This is the first of our kicks. As with all the more obvious martial pieces in the form, it is important not to become hasty and impulsive. These movements have enormous therapeutic value, but only when performed slowly. Do not try to kick too high, either, as this will only introduce unwanted tension.

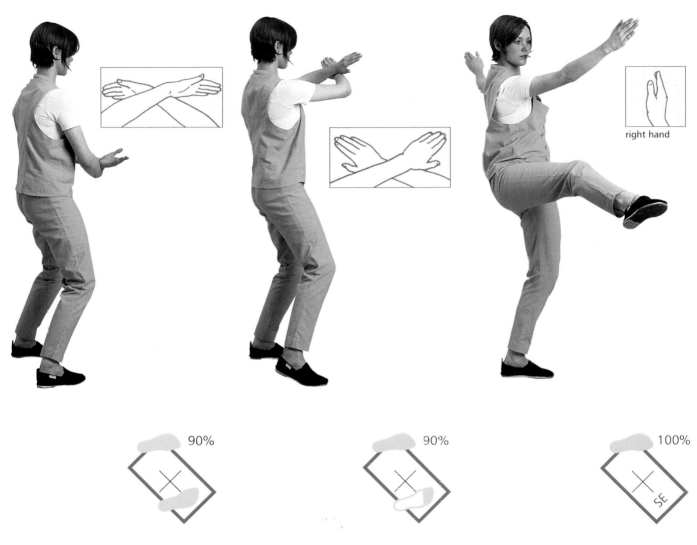

right hand

90%   90%   100%

83 *Breathe In*
Turn in your right foot by pivoting on the heel to go slightly pigeon-toed. At the same time drop your right arm and cross your wrists, left wrist over right at waist level. In the process, your left hand will want to execute a little clockwise circular movement to drop down onto your right wrist, just as the right arm descends. The hands should be fairly flat and blade-like, but not tense.

83a *In-breath Finishes*
Now raise your crossed hands to about chin-height. As the arms rise in preparation for the next phase, the wrists roll over so that the palms change from their inward-facing position to face outward, northeast. Also the right foot begins to turn back toward the southeast; this is achieved by pivoting on the toes, which automatically lifts the knee and prepares you for the forthcoming kick.

84 *Breathe Out*
Continue to pivot on your right toes and then raise your knee as you separate your hands to draw a large arc in the air: your right hand goes forward, and your left hand goes back behind. Then, bringing up your shin, kick out to the southeast with your right foot. In this case, if you were actually kicking something it would be the toes that make contact, hence the name "Kick with Toes."

Pat the Horse on the Left

In tai chi, after each kick we are urged to take an in-breath with the knee still raised before proceeding into the next move. This cultivates balance and *strength, since any tendency to lunge forward or topple after the kick exposes a weakness in our root. This can then be corrected by further practice.*

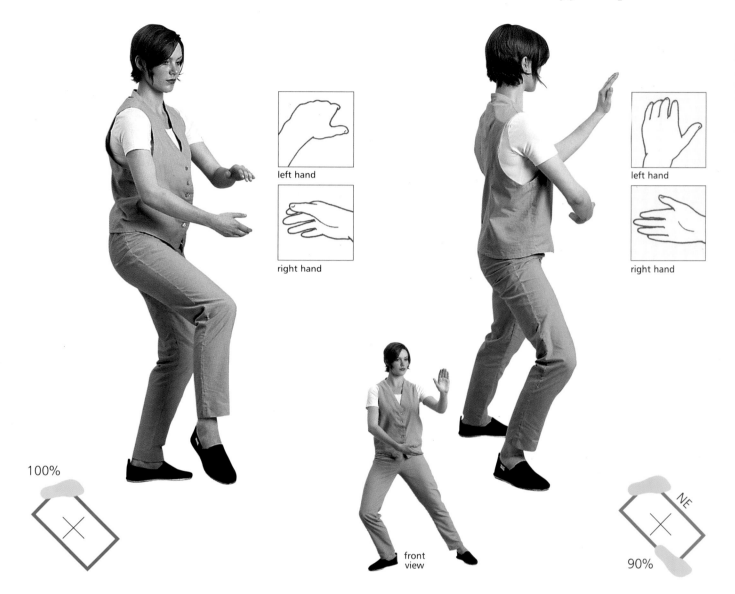

left hand

right hand

100%

front view

left hand

right hand

NE

90%

85 *Breathe In*
Still keeping your knee up, drop the shin and lower your arms inward just a little. You are going to step down in a moment into another Pat Horse, this time on the left side. However, whereas for Pat the Horse on the Right your weight was in the back leg, here it is going to be in the front leg. Remember it like this: the first time you meet the horse you are cautious, so you keep back, but here, the second time around, you are more confident, so your weight goes forward.

86 *Breathe Out*
Place your right foot down just a little ahead of your left with your toes pointing out to the southeast. Then, bringing your weight forward, place your left palm out to the northeast to rest on the horse's flank, while turning your right palm up, as if holding an apple for the horse to eat. As with the previous Pat Horse, your arms move into position across your body, the left hand sweeping over from the center toward the north, while the right hand pulls back from the north toward the center. Once again, allow this kind of dexterity to develop by degrees.

68

Separate Hands and Kick With Left Toes

Another kick with the toes comes next. Remember with all kicks it is the knee that rises first, then the rest of the leg springs up into position. Do not worry if your balance lets you down at the start. With practice this will improve. Also, never kick so high as to introduce unnecessary tension.

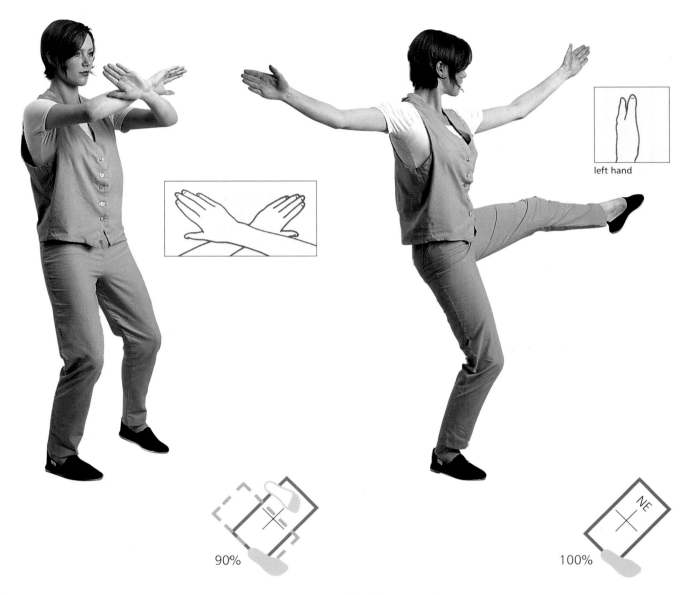

left hand

90%

100%

87 *Breathe In*
Step up a little with your left foot to bring it almost level with your right and pivot on the heel to go slightly pigeon-toed. At the same time drop your left arm and cross your hands, right wrist over left, palms facing in at the level of your waist. This time your right hand has to execute a little counterclockwise circular movement to drop down on to your left wrist. Then once again, as in step number 83a, lift your hands to about chin-height, rotating your wrists outward as you go, so that your palms finish up facing roughly southeast.

88 *Breathe Out*
Pivot on your left toes and lift your knee as you separate your hands once more to draw a large arc in the air: your left hand goes forward, northeast, and your right hand travels back behind, roughly southwest. Then kick – that is, lift the rest of your left leg and project your foot out to the southeast. Do not forget that this is another *toe* kick, so there is a stretch along the front aspect of the leg and foot. Direct your gaze outward – do not look down – and try to keep your hands flat and blade-like, so that the whole movement has a crisp appearance.

69

Turn and Kick With Heel

The next movement involves a turn on the right heel that is often done without actually placing the left foot down at all. However, here we follow the simplified version, which even advanced practitioners of tai chi will avail themselves of at times – for instance, *on a difficult surface like sand. These kicks are naturally some of the most spectacular and impressive movements in the form – but do not get carried away! They do not need to be excessively high, and should certainly never be done at speed.*

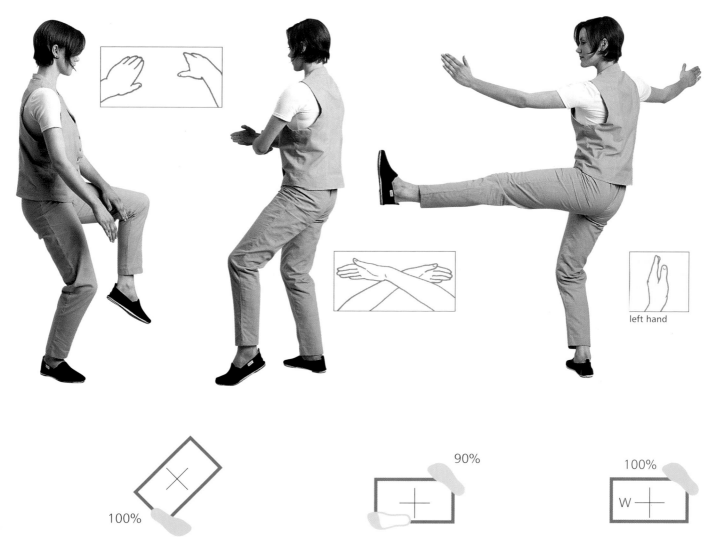

left hand

100%

90%

100%

89 *Breathe In*
Drop your shin, keeping your knee up, and lower your arms slowly, your left arm coming down vertically across your center, and your right arm coming to settle just to the outside of your right hip. You are about to turn on your right heel to face your hips and shoulders west; as you go, let your right wrist cross over the left. This will happen naturally with the momentum of the turn, if your arm is relaxed.

89a *In-breath Finishes*
Rotate your waist counterclockwise and place your left foot down behind, toes first. Shifting your weight momentarily into your left foot, pivot on your right heel to get your toes pointing northwest and then return your weight to your right foot as you raise your left knee again. Your hands should have crossed by now, right wrist over left, and you then roll them up to your chin, as before.

90 *Breathe Out*
With your knee raised and your hips and shoulders facing west, lift your shin and project your left foot forward to kick. If you were making contact with anything, it would be the sole or heel of the left foot that would do so. This is a different feel from the previous kicks – here there is a stretch along the back of the leg. Your hands, meanwhile, separate in a graceful arc, the left hand going forward.

Brush Left Knee and Push

It is important to recognize the yin phase (in-breath) of the movements that follow. A common error is to concentrate simply on the yang parts, the pushes, *and not on the yielding, gathering-up phases that precede them. Take time for the inhalations, and allow the body to rotate freely as you go.*

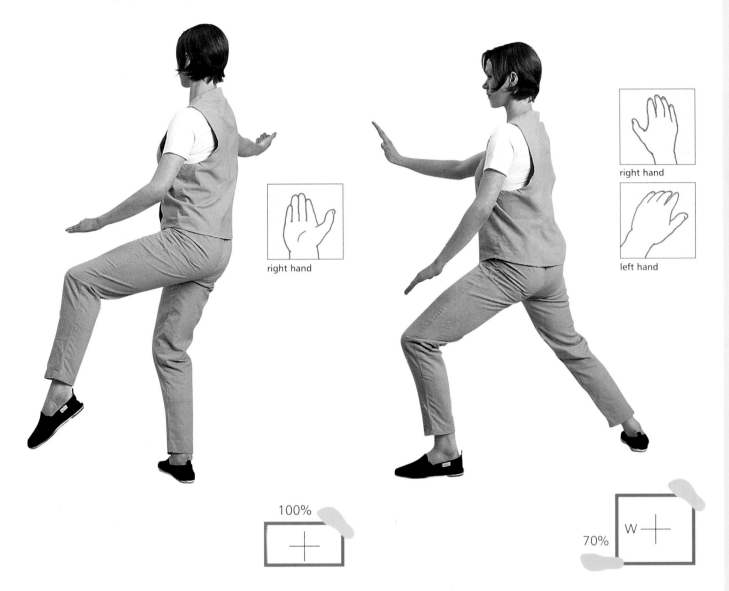

right hand

right hand

left hand

100%

70% W

91 *Breathe In*
We are about to drop down into a movement already encountered in Section Three *(see page 36).* After the kick with the left foot, drop your shin, and with your knee still up, circle back a little with your right hand, palm facing up; let your gaze follow your hand as it goes. This deliberate pause, still on the one leg and during which we take an inhalation, really tests our balance and our ability to stay calm and steady after the impetus of the kick itself. Otherwise, it can be tempting to simply lunge forward into the next position, which is not good tai chi.

92 *Breathe Out*
Set your left foot down, heel first, good and wide, and brush (remember the distance) your left knee with the palm of your left hand. Bend your knee to bring your weight forward as your right palm pushes past your right ear and then onward to the west. Make sure your palm finishes centrally, not way out to your side, and at about chest height, no higher. Relax your left hand after the brush-knee component of this movement, so that your energy can focus itself into your right palm. *(See page 36 for a front view of this stance.)*

Brush Right Knee and Push

These particular movements are illustrative of a very important principle in tai chi – that is, the main action is always focused in one hand at a time. So it is brush the knee first and then push. There is space between these two components; they do not occur together.

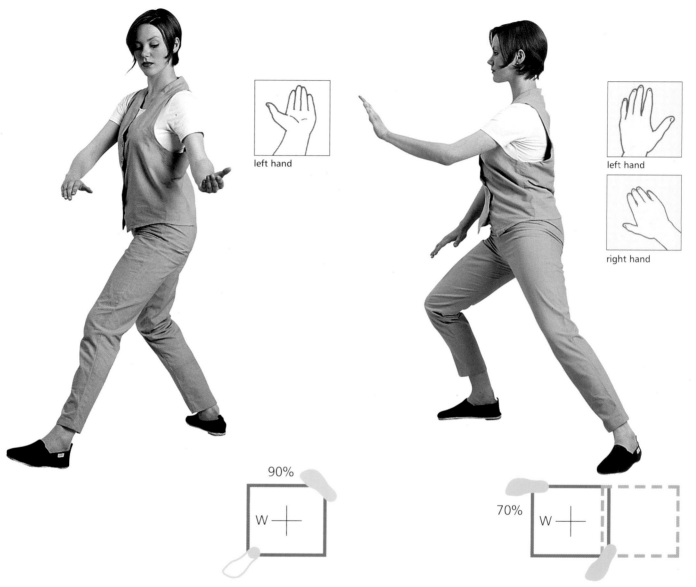

left hand

left hand

right hand

90%

W

70%

W

93 *Breathe In*
We are now going to repeat the brush knee and push sequence, but this time on the other side. Begin by establishing the yin phase properly by sitting back and turning out your left toes. Drop your right arm to the center while circling the left palm back behind your shoulder, palm up, letting your gaze follow your hand as it goes. Try to establish an energy connection between your hands as you rotate your waist, counterclockwise, to accommodate the backward journey of your left hand. Above all, take your time.

94 *Breathe Out*
With your weight settled in your left side, step out west with your right foot, heel first, and bend your knee to bring your weight forward. As you step, brush your right knee with your right palm (keeping distance between the two), your hand traveling from left to right in a sweeping motion. Then push out with your left palm toward the west. Although it remains near your thigh, your right hand becomes relaxed after the brush-knee, so that your energy can focus itself more into your left palm. Your hips and shoulders should be facing west.

Brush Left Knee and Punch Low

This, as the name implies, is very similar to Brush Left Knee and Push. The main difference is that instead of pushing with the right palm at the end of the movement, you form a fist in the right hand and then punch downward, dropping the body relatively low.

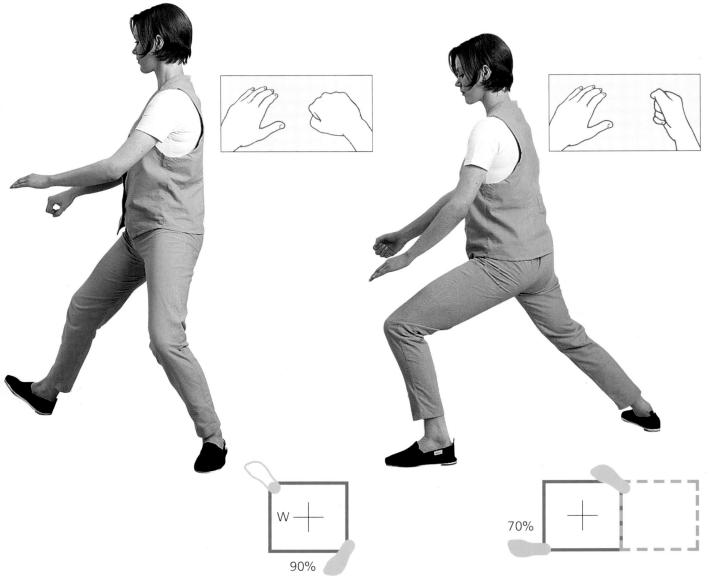

95 *Breathe In*
Begin by shifting your weight into your back leg to enable you to turn out the toes of your front foot by pivoting on your right heel. At the same time your left hand circles down and your right hand forms a fist, knuckles up, by your right hip. You may recall that when we encountered the preparation for the punch back on page 39, the knuckles of the hand initially faced downward. Here, they face upward due to the low angle at which the punch is directed. It feels more comfortable this way.

96 *Breathe Out*
Now put the whole of your right foot down and step out west with your left foot, heel first, and bend your knee. As you do so, your left palm brushes over your left thigh. Then project your fist forward and down a little, following it with your gaze, the fist itself rotating as it goes from the knuckles-up position to finish with the thumb side uppermost. Again, compare this to the final stages of the punch on pages 39–40. Try not to bend or lean forward as you punch; rather, just lengthen your stance and sink downward instead.

SEVEN

Rotating and Turning

Here the emphasis is on rotational movements – work that involves twisting and turning, particularly beneficial for the lower organs of the abdomen and for the reproductive and urinary systems. This is mainly found in a lengthy sequence called Four Corners, sometimes also known as Fair Lady Works at Shuttles, as the arm movements loosely resemble those of someone working at an old-fashioned loom.

Grasp the Bird's Tail

We begin and indeed finish this section with a repetition of the Chorus – Grasp the Bird's Tail right through to the Single Whip. Try not to speed up these *movements simply because you are already familiar with them. Keep the rhythm and breathing at a constant level throughout.*

left hand

right hand

90%

W

70%

W

97 *Breathe In*
From your Brush Left Knee and Punch Low at the end of the last section *(see left)*, shift your weight back again, this time into the right side, and turn out your left toes. Then as the weight starts to drift forward into your left leg again, and as your left foot begins to flatten on to the ground, rotate your waist counterclockwise and, from a relatively low position on your left-hand side, pick up a ball, left hand on top, right hand underneath. Keep your back upright as your waist turns.

98 *Breathe Out*
Rotate your waist back to the center and step forward with your right foot, heel first, and bend your knee. Bring the ball with you, the ball getting smaller and smaller as you go until you can "Grasp the Bird's Tail" – just like the movement you have done before *(see page 27)*. Again, you finish up with the right arm slanting upward and the fingers of the left hand pointing at the right palm. The "bird" is held in your right hand, while the left hand rests on the long tail feathers behind. Remember to keep your right knee over your right toes.

75

Chorus (continued)

Here is the rest of the Chorus, illustrated on a smaller scale since you should by now be familiar with the movements. If in any doubt, refer to pages 27–31 where the whole sequence is described in detail. Do *not forget to keep your knees soft at all times – resist the temptation to lock the left knee when the weight goes into the rear leg. Also, remember that the spine remains upright, not leaning forward or back.*

Rollback and Press

99 *Breathe In* **99a** *In-breath Finishes* **100** *Breathe Out*

Separate Hands and Push

101 *Breathe In* **102** *Breathe Out*

NOTE: *It is important not to treat these movements with indifference simply because they are familiar. Do not rush them! Patient acceptance of the familiar is a measure of your commitment to daily practice. After all, the entire form will soon be familiar to you and yet, hopefully, you will not want to rush it – or even abandon it – just because of this.*

Chorus (continued)

The constant repetition of movements which have become totally assimilated into the sub-conscious, and therefore do not require any conscious thought, is precisely what enables us to let go of the rational mind and approach the quality that the Chinese call Wu Wei ("no mind"), the sense of "moving meditation" for which the practice of tai chi is so highly prized.

Single Whip

103 *Breathe In*   **104** *Breathe Out*   **105** *Breathe In*

106 *Breathe Out*   **107** *Breathe In*   **108** *Breathe Out*

Four Corners (Number One)

We are about to embark on the Four Corners sequence, a collection of four tiny routines each virtually identical to the other and performed in an elegant rotational sequence. The main variation between them is in the footwork, and even this follows a basic pattern of pivoting on heels and toes.

right hand

left hand

90%

90%

109 *Breathe In*
From the Single Whip place your weight into your right side and turn on your left heel to point the toes inward. Your waist rotates clockwise at the same time. Meanwhile let go of the crane's beak and rotate your right palm up and inward, so that it is facing your left shoulder. Your right forearm then comes back toward you to a near-vertical position, and your left hand drops to your center, as if to cup the right elbow at a distance.

110 *Breathe Out*
Shift the weight back across into your left side just as you begin your exhalation. Then with your waist still turning in its clockwise direction, lift your right foot from the ground and place it down again with your toes pointing roughly toward the west. Finally bring all of your weight into your right side once more by bending your right knee and sinking most of your weight into it.

Four Corners (Number One – continued)

There are many variations on how precisely the hands should be placed during the Four Corners turns — some, for example, advocate keeping the palms facing out. Here, however, we rotate them inward to set up an agreeable spiraling experience for the wrists and hands as the movement unfolds.

right hand

left hand

100%

SW

70%

111 *Breathe In*
With all your weight in your right side, draw your left toes in a little closer to your right foot and prepare to step out toward the southwest. At this stage your arms are starting to open – that is, your palms begin to rotate outward and your lower arm begins to rise. Think of the left palm running up the outside of the right forearm, at a distance – not touching – and gradually, let your body expand with the in-breath.

112 *Breathe Out*
Step into a wide 70/30 stance toward the southwest with your left foot, heel first, and bend your knee to bring your weight forward. At the same time raise your left hand and rotate it outward to about head height and then rotate your right palm and push forward at about chest height. If necessary, adjust your back foot to a comfortable position by pivoting on your right heel. Your left knee should be over your left toes at the conclusion of this movement – the first of the four corners. Your hips and shoulders should be facing southwest.

Four Corners (Number Two)

For the next corner we have to execute a long three-quarter turn, right around to the southeast. This is based on a long clockwise rotation of the body and *is achieved through a similar combination of turning on heels and toes as we encountered on corner number one.*

left hand

right hand

front view

90%

SW

90%

113 *Breathe In*
Begin by emptying the weight from your left side so that you can pivot on your left heel to point the toes as far toward the north as possible. Rotate your hands inward and draw back your arms once again – your left palm facing your right shoulder, and your right palm, having dropped to your center, heading toward your left elbow to present the same cupping configuration as before, only this time on the opposite side. This alternation of sides occurs on each of the corners.

114 *Breathe Out*
Transfer all your weight into your left foot as you continue to turn your waist north and then raise your right heel to pivot on your right toes so that the right foot is also pointing in a northerly direction. This helps to shift the body around even further on its long journey toward the southeast. Remember to move from the center of your body, as well as with the aid of the feet. Also, do make sure you keep your shoulders relaxed and your body upright as you go.

Four Corners (Number Two – continued)

Four Corners (Number Two – continued)

As you will certainly have discovered by now, there are two whole breaths allocated to each corner, and this encourages us to really take our time and relish the subtle shifting of weight from side to side, one foot to the other, which facilitates the large turning movements required.

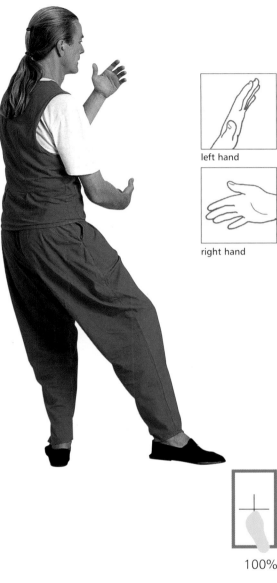

left hand

right hand

100%

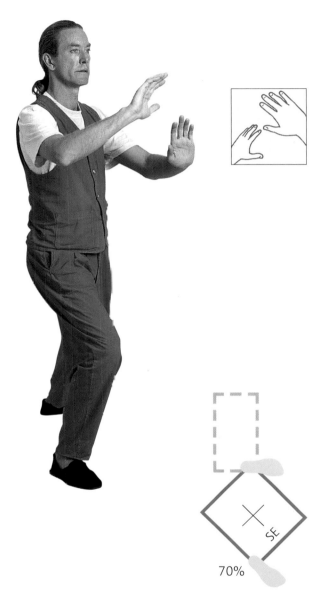

SE

70%

115 *Breathe In*
Lift your right foot entirely from the ground and keep turning your waist clockwise. You are preparing to step around to the southeast into a wide stance, and so at this stage your arms start to open again, the palms beginning to rotate outward and the lower arm beginning to rise, all very gradually. Think of the right palm running up the outside of the left forearm at a distance. Let the inhalation open your shoulders for you, and keep your back straight.

116 *Breathe Out*
Complete the turn by stepping out with your right foot into a wide stance to the southeast. Make contact with the heel first and then slowly set your foot down flat on the ground by bending your knee. Do not forget to adjust your left heel to a comfortable position as soon as the weight settles in your right side. Meanwhile your arms continue to expand – right hand to head height, palm out, while you push slightly forward with your left palm at chest height. That's corner number two – hips, shoulders and palms all facing southeast.

Four Corners (Number Three)

The rotations of the palms in Four Corners, along with the contraction and expansion of the lower limbs, can be compared to the closing and opening of a flower – something unhurried and wholly organic. This movement is also a perfect example of yin and yang (yielding and pushing) in action.

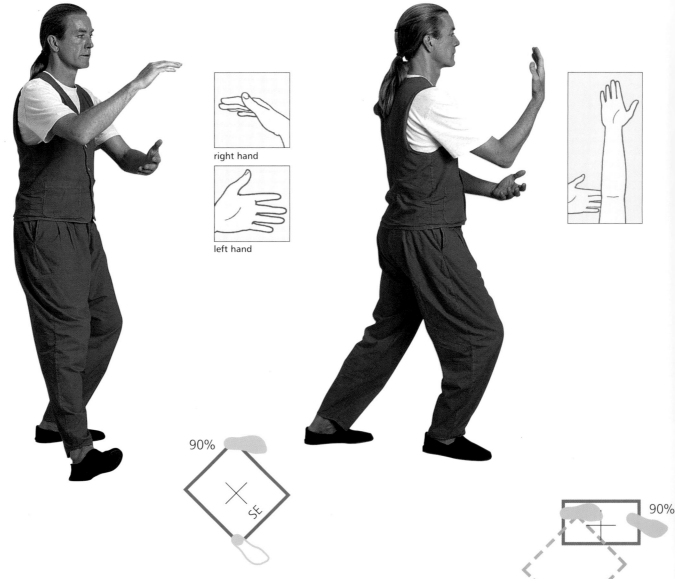

right hand

left hand

90%

90%

117 *Breathe In*
The approach to the third corner is more direct than for the previous two, taking us straight across to the northeast. Begin by emptying the weight from your right foot then rotate your arms slightly inward once again. This time, the right palm rotates to face the left shoulder – the forearm moving closer to the body in a near-vertical position. The left hand, meanwhile, drops to the center, as if to cup the right elbow from a distance.

118 *Breathe Out*
With all of your weight in your left side, lift your right foot and step forward and slightly across to place it down flat on the ground just in front of your left foot. Try not to step in too close; there should be plenty of space between your feet. Once your right foot is on the ground, bring your weight forward by bending your right knee. At this stage your head and shoulders should be facing roughly east.

Four Corners (Number Three – continued)

Four Corners has one golden rule: at the end of each corner, the side with the leading leg always has the higher arm. So if you are stepping forward with the right leg, the right arm finishes the higher of the two. The same applies to the other side; if the left leg is leading, the left arm is higher than the right.

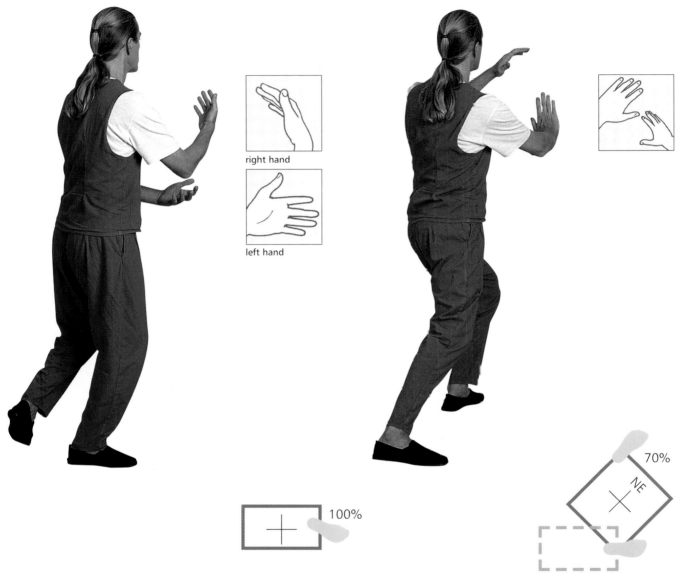

right hand

left hand

100%

70%

NE

119 *Breathe In*

Sink into your right side as you prepare to step out toward the northeast by raising your left heel. At this stage your arms start to open out again, the palms gradually beginning to rotate outward and the lower arm beginning to rise. Think of the left palm running up the outside of the right forearm at a distance. Let your body expand with the breath. Also, start to rotate your center so that your hips and shoulders begin to face northeast. Try not to look down too much.

120 *Breathe Out*

With all your weight settled in the right side, step out with your left heel to the northeast and bend your knee to bring your weight forward. Continue rotating and raising your left hand to head height, palm out, and then push slightly forward with your right palm at chest-height. If necessary, adjust the back foot to a comfortable position by pivoting on your right heel. That concludes the third corner; left foot, hips, shoulders and palms all face northeast.

Four Corners (Number Four)

For the final corner we need to execute another long three-quarter turn, this time around to the northwest. As always, concentrate on shifting the weight from side to side as you go; in other words, whenever a foot turns, whether on the heel or the toes, make sure it is empty of weight.

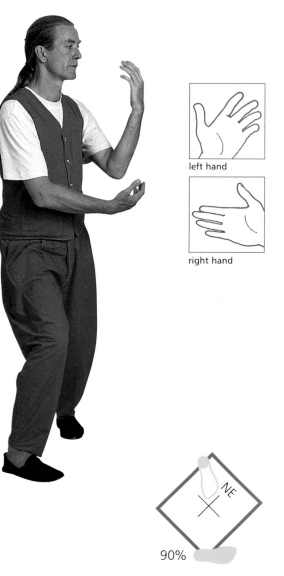

left hand

right hand

121 *Breathe In*
Start by transferring your weight back into the right side. Lower your arms and pivot on your left heel to point the toes as near south as possible before setting your foot down. Rotate your hands inward and draw your arms back once again – the left palm facing your right shoulder and the right palm, having dropped to your center, near your left elbow. As you rotate your body, try to cultivate a "corkscrew" feeling in the lower limbs and groin; this is most beneficial to the internal organs. But stay relaxed!

122 *Breathe Out*
Transfer all your weight into the left side, sink into your left foot and then raise your right heel to pivot on your right toes so that your right foot is also pointing in a roughly southerly direction. Rotate your waist clockwise as you go. All this helps to shift the body around still further on its long journey to the northwest, which is where the fourth corner is taking us. Keep your shoulders relaxed and your body upright as you go and again, except during the very early stages of learning, avoid looking down at your feet.

Four Corners (Number Four – continued)

With regard to the very obvious expanding and contracting rhythm of each corner – especially noticeable in the arms and hands – try to make this *a gradual process, so that the arms are never static but rather constantly rotating, lifting or sinking during their passage from one corner to the next.*

left hand

right hand

00%

70%

NW

123 *Breathe In*
Lift your right foot entirely from the ground and keep turning your waist clockwise. You are preparing to step around to the northwest into a wide stance, and at this stage your arms start to open again, the palms beginning to rotate outward and the lower arm beginning to rise, all very slowly and smoothly. Again, think of the right palm running up the outside of the left forearm at a distance. Let the inhalation expand your shoulders as your arms start to uncurl.

124 *Breathe Out*
Still turning your waist, step out with your right foot into a wide stance to the northwest. Make contact with the heel first and then slowly set your foot down flat on the ground by bending your knee. Do not forget to adjust your left heel to a comfortable position as soon as the weight settles in your right side. Meanwhile, your arms continue to spiral out – right hand to head height, palm out, while you push slightly forward with your left palm at chest height. That's corner number four, the final one, with your hips and shoulders facing northwest.

85

Ward Off Left

After the Four Corners sequence we meet with more repeated movements. Among these is the final Chorus, but just before that we have the Ward Off *movement, again a repetition, and one that we first encountered early on in the form in Section Two (see page 26).*

right hand

left hand

left hand

90%

70%

125 *Breathe In*
Rotate your palms inward slightly and cup the right elbow. Your waist is going to rotate again, but this time in a counterclockwise direction. Help this along by pivoting a little, first on your right heel and then on your left toes ready to step toward the south into a wide 70/30 stance with your left foot. As always, check your balance before taking the final step. Meanwhile the hand energy begins to focus largely in your right palm, ready to "stroke" downward.

126 *Breathe Out*
Step out to the south with your left foot, heel first, and bend your knee to bring your weight forward. Your waist continues turning counterclockwise toward the south, so that your hips and shoulders face forward in a typical wide 70/30 stance. Simultaneously the left arm rises so that the forearm becomes horizontal, palm facing the chest, while the right hand drops to the side. Try to sense the energy connection between the palms as they pass. Finally do not forget to pivot inward a little on your right heel to release any tension in the back knee.

Chorus

After Ward Off Left comes the final Chorus of the form, beginning with Grasp the Bird's Tail and going right through to the Single Whip, illustrated here once again on a smaller scale. If you are in any doubt about how to perform these movements, refer to pages 27–31, where they are described in detail.

Grasp the Bird's Tail

127
Breathe In

128
Breathe Out

Rollback and Press

129
Breathe In

129a
In-breath Finishes

130
Breathe Out

NOTE: *A common error made by students learning Rollback and Press is to sway from side to side as the knees bend, transferring the weight forward or back. Always try, therefore, to keep your body on the midline, between your feet, as you move. Do not lean excessively over to the right as you go forward, for instance, or over to the left as you sit back.*

Separate Hands and Push

131
Breathe In

132
Breathe Out

Single Whip

133
Breathe In

134
Breathe Out

135
Breathe In

136
Breathe Out

137
Breathe In

138
Breathe Out

EIGHT

The Closing Sequence

Whereas the early part of the form was all about developing balance and spatial awareness, here at the conclusion we learn to integrate these skills with the qualities of agility and strength. The character of the movements in this closing sequence is particularly flamboyant, full of turns and extravagant sweeps of the arms – at times quite martial in character, while at others quite breathtakingly beautiful.

Snake Creeps Down

A common error here is to bend forward or compress the body in the interest of trying to squat down as low as possible (which is not really necessary).

You must try to avoid this. It is usually very difficult for those of us with stiff hips to get down – so do not despair! In time you will become more flexible.

left hand

left hand

90%

90%

139 *Breathe In*
From the Single Whip at the conclusion of the last section, we go straight into Snake Creeps Down once again *(see also page 63)*. Begin to lengthen your stance by sliding back with your right foot to point your toes southwest. Then sit back into your right leg and turn a little on your left heel to point your toes inward, roughly southeast. At the same time, draw your left hand back a little toward your chest, rotating the palm to face inward.

140 *Breathe Out*
Squat down into your rear leg, your front leg remaining relatively straight with just a slight bend to the knee as you go Simultaneously allow your left hand to swoop down and then to thrust forward again, fingers first, close to the ground and with the palm facing south. Your hand continues on past your left foot, which then straightens out to point east once more. Remember to keep your body as upright as possible when you sink down. Always work within your limitations and stay relaxed and comfortable at all times.

Step Forward to Seven Stars

The "seven stars" in this movement are the seven most visible stars of the Big Dipper. If you look at this stance in profile, the shape formed is that of the constellation known as Ursa Major, which, in terms of Chinese mythology, has great significance. This is partly due to the fact that two of its stars always point toward the North Star or polestar, a special point of stillness in the sky.

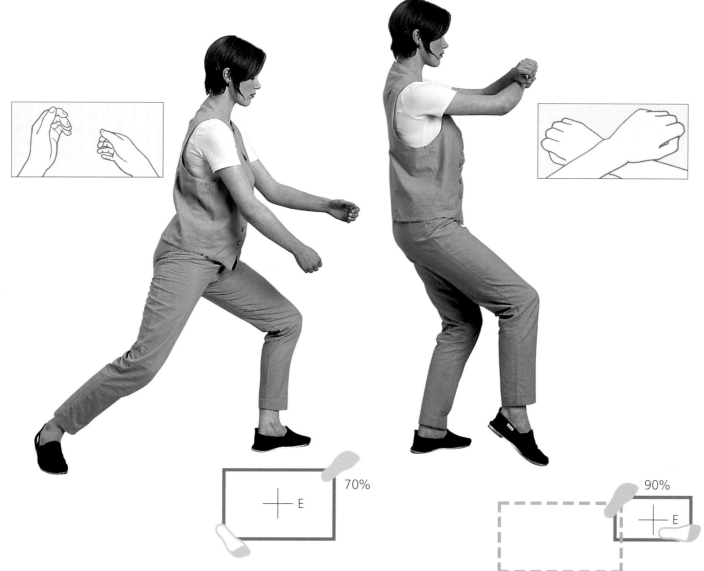

70%

90%

141 *Breathe In*
Raise the body a little and bring your weight forward. This releases the weight from your right foot and enables you to turn it inward again to a comfortable position. Then shift your weight back yet again and turn out your left foot by pivoting on the heel. Finally bend your left knee and bring your weight forward into the left side once more, ready to step out at any time with the right foot. Meanwhile your arms move in toward the center, your wrists ready to cross as you prepare for the next position.

142 *Breathe Out*
With all your weight in your left side, step up with your right foot and place it down in a narrow toe stance to the east. As you do this, cross your wrists, left over right, the hands having shaped themselves into two fists. Initially the palm-sides of the hands are facing you. But then, as you bring your body forward, the wrists roll so that the knuckle side of the hands finishes facing you. This rolling movement also takes the two fists up to about the level of your chin.

Step Back to Ride the Tiger

The tiger is a creature that appears quite frequently in the naming of the tai chi movements, just as it does in Chinese art and literature. A symbol of *strength and vital energy, it is also the mightiest of opponents. Our greatest strength, therefore, and our greatest adversary both lie within ourselves.*

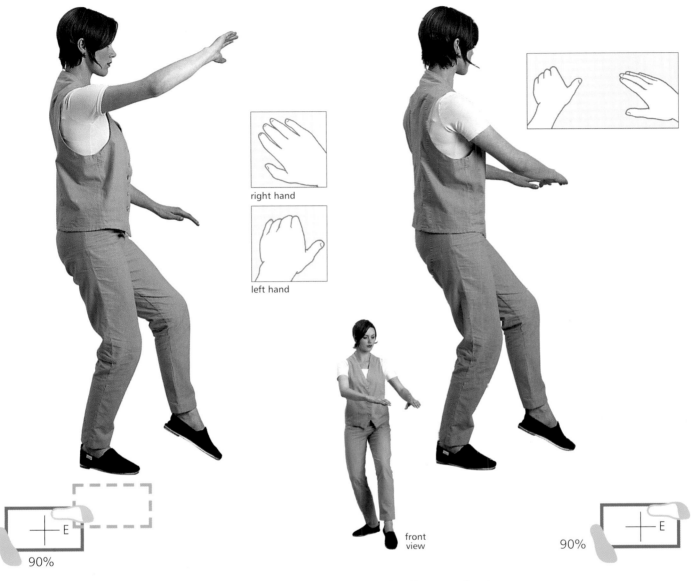

right hand

left hand

front view

90%

90%

143 *Breathe In*
Uncross your wrists and open your hands. Then, keeping most of your weight in your left side for the time being, step back with your right foot, making contact with your toes first, and bring your weight into it. Next create a narrow toe stance on the left by raising your left foot and setting it down again properly aligned to the east. Your hands, meanwhile, separate out – the left hand dropping to the center, and the right hand curving down and then spiraling up again to about head-height, with the palm facing toward the southeast.

144 *Breathe Out*
Very slowly allow your left hand to drift north to settle above and just to the outside of your left hip. Then allow your right hand, the palm outward-facing, to swoop over and then down in a graceful arc, closing in once again toward the left hand. Both palms face downward at the conclusion of this movement, and the fingers of the right hand point at the left. It is important during this circular journey of the right hand that you do not raise or tense your right shoulder.

Sweep the Lotus and Crescent Kick

The lotus is an aquatic plant and, like the rose in Western culture, possesses a certain mystical significance – in this case, having its roots in the mud while its flower is high above, resplendent upon the surface of the water, and so largely invisible to the roots themselves.

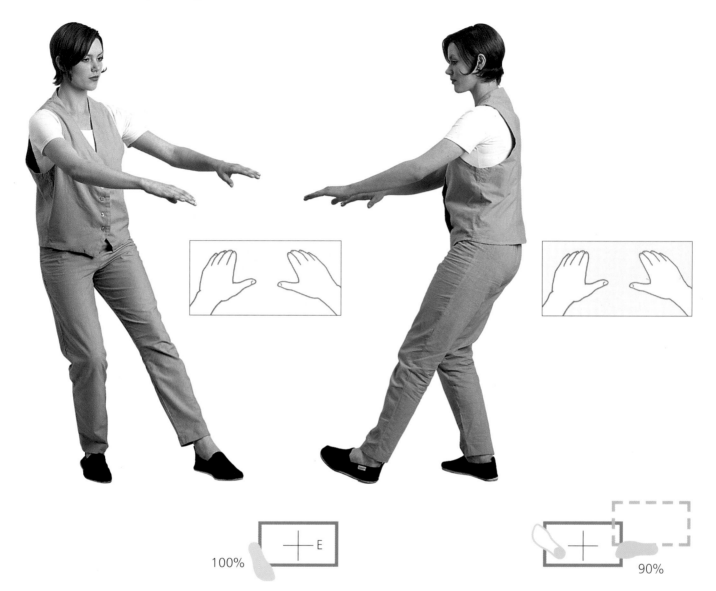

100%

90%

145 *Breathe In*
With all of your weight now in the right side, straighten out your left leg a little and raise it from the ground. Then, using the momentum of your left leg and your arms, which are held out in front of you, sweep your body around in a clockwise direction, turning all the while on the ball of your right foot. This, rather irreverently, is the actual "sweeping" of the lotus from the surface of the pool, the left foot very close to the water.

145a *Still Breathing In*
This movement is illustrated here in detail, since beginners often find it a struggle to perform at first. In fact, what is taking place is a whole 360-degree turn; the halfway stage is shown above. At this point, you need to set your left heel down on "dry land" to the west and prepare for the continuation of your turn by shifting your weight into it. Try not to flail your arms in all directions as you go, but rather keep them steady and softly energized throughout.

Sweep the Lotus and Crescent Kick (continued)

The Crescent Kick is the yang phase of the previous movement – Sweep the Lotus – and is, in fact, often called the Lotus Kick. Another reason for the lotus association: here is the spinning appearance that the petals of this particular flower tend to have in the wind.

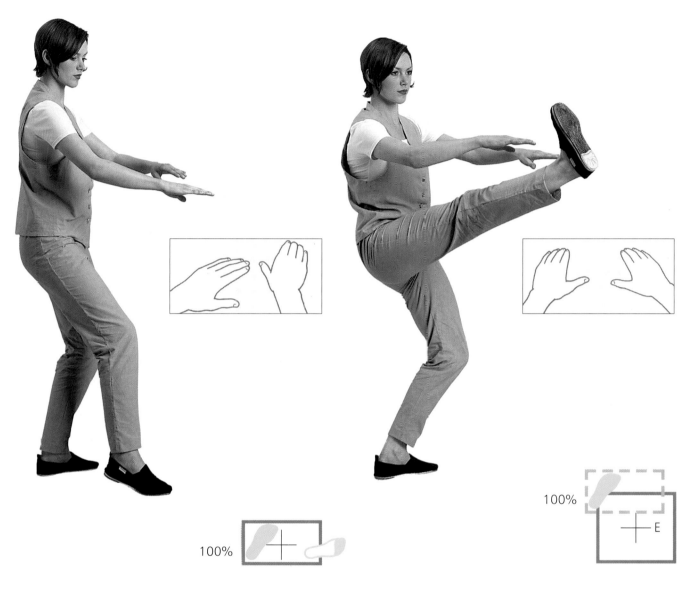

100%

100%

E

145b *In-breath Finishes*
This turn often needs to be accomplished fairly fast, especially for beginners of tai chi, so do not be tempted to perform it slowly simply because the in-breath is demonstrated here in three stages. Continue your turn by using the ball of your right foot and the heel of your left in combination to bring your body around to face the east once more, in a relatively compact narrow toe stance. The forearms, meanwhile, continue to remain horizontal, as they have done throughout the turn.

146 *Breathe Out*
Allow your forearms, still horizontal, to drift a little to your right. Raise your right knee and then, as the shin also comes up to create a level, horizontal aspect to the leg, kick out in an arc – a crescent shape – toward the southeast. Here the "kick" is actually the sweeping motion made by your leg as it swings round from the east to the southeast. If you were physically making contact with anything, it would be the outer edge of your foot that would do so. As your leg sweeps to your right, your hands, still with the forearms horizontal, sweep very slightly to the left to finish about center.

Sweep the Lotus and Crescent Kick (continued)

You may well have noticed by now that the kicks are always executed on an exhalation. The crescent kick is no exception. After the kick is complete, however, *we do not simply fall impatiently into the next move, but rather take another slow inhalation and steady the mind and body before proceeding further.*

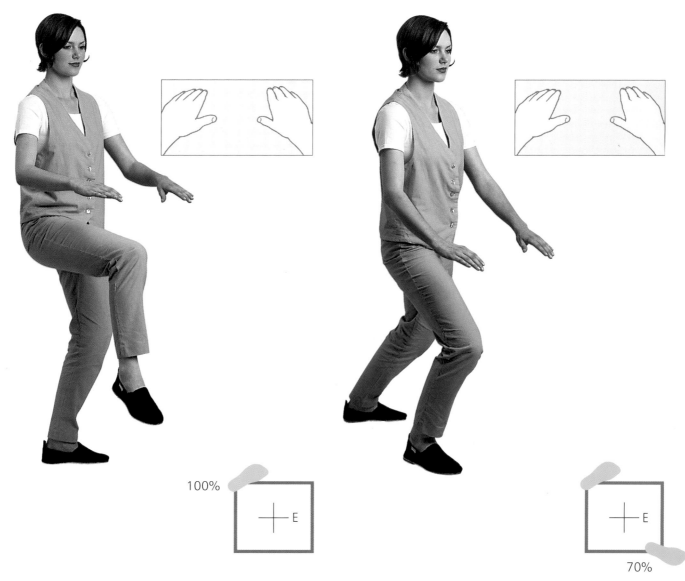

100%

+E

70%

147 *Breathe In*
After executing Sweep the Lotus and Crescent Kick, it is enough for beginners to conclude this rather flamboyant sequence with a dignified and steady descent back down to the ground. But for those who have been practicing the form for some time, there are certain refinements that can be made. For example, before setting your foot down, try turning your waist very slightly to the right to align your body with your right thigh. Your arms may also want to drift back across to settle above your thigh.

148 *Breathe Out*
Set your right foot down to point southeast in a wide 70/30 stance, making contact with your heel first and bending the knee to bring your weight slowly forward. Sink down and enjoy the exhalation fully. At the same time, start to shape your hands into two loose fists level with each other at about hip-height, as though you were gently clasping a thin railing between your hands. This is the "bow" mentioned in the title of the next movement, though for the time being try not to get too caught up in images. And keep those shoulders relaxed!

Bend the Bow and Shoot the Tiger

The image here is of someone bending a bow or staff that has been thrust into the ground. With this, the joints of the shoulders, elbows and wrists produce many pleasing curves and spirals along the way, but make sure that your shoulders do not tense up or rise at the same time. Stay relaxed.

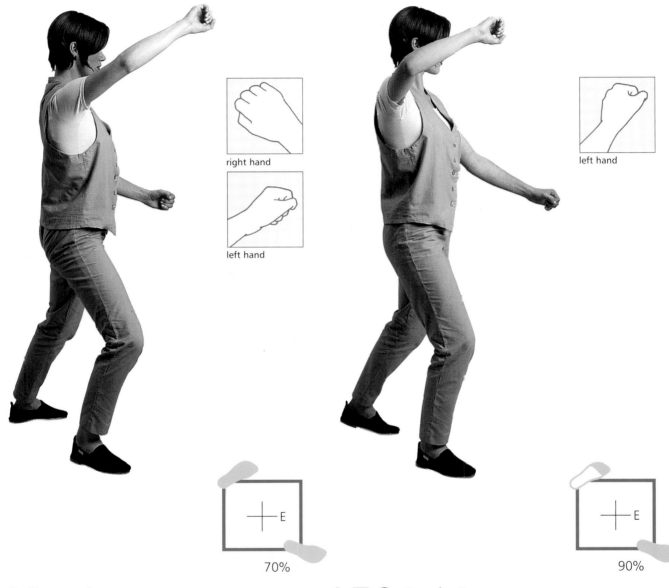

right hand

left hand

left hand

70%

90%

149 *Breathe In*
With most of your weight forward in your right side, glide the right fist up and across in a graceful sweeping curve to about head-height and with the knuckles turned inward to face north at the top of the movement. This means that your arm has a gentle twist or spiral shape along its length. In other words, your hand should rotate as it rises, from a palm-down position to a palm-out position. Any rotation of this kind has its origin at the elbow, but even the shoulder rotates a little as well.

150 *Breathe Out*
Allow your waist to turn clockwise a little and, with the knuckles still turned inward, draw your right fist back to a position close to the side of your head, while projecting your left fist forward just a moment later; this is the "bending of the bow." The action of the left hand here is unusual, being more of a sideways, "grazing" kind of motion – that is, outward as well as forward. Finally, let the back foot leave the ground a little by raising your left knee.

Step Forward, Parry and Punch

As mentioned earlier, the short yang form is normally structured and taught in two parts, each one finishing with the same sequence of movements.

And we have, therefore, already met with these at the end of Section Three (traditionally the end of the first part of the short yang form: see pages 39–43).

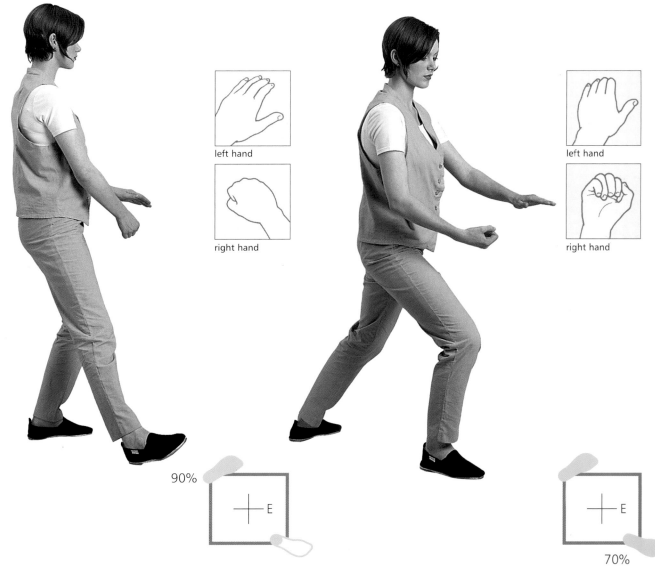

left hand

right hand

90%

E

left hand

right hand

70%

151 *Breathe In*
Allow your weight to "rock" back into the rear leg as it makes contact with the ground again, toes first, of course, because this is a step backward. Then, with your weight firmly in your left side, let go of the fist in your left hand while allowing your arms to drop, both fairly central – the left hand with its open palm almost horizontal and the right hand, still with its fist intact, hovering at about the height of the navel.

152 *Breathe Out*
The right foot is already forward, so there is no need for the first "step" of the Parry and Punch sequence as first described on page 39 (remember – we counted three steps throughout the movement). Instead simply lift your right foot for a moment and then set it down again with your toes pointing well out, providing a good wide base for the next stance. As you do this, thrust your right fist around to your right side, palm side uppermost, sink into your right leg and bend your knee. This is equivalent to the second step of the movement.

Step Forward, Parry and Punch (continued)

As you approach the end of the form, it is tempting to speed up, and a common error with this sequence is to get carried away with the idea of the punch.

Try not to become impulsive or aggressive with this; remember, throughout the whole form the tempo remains slow and even, calm and easy.

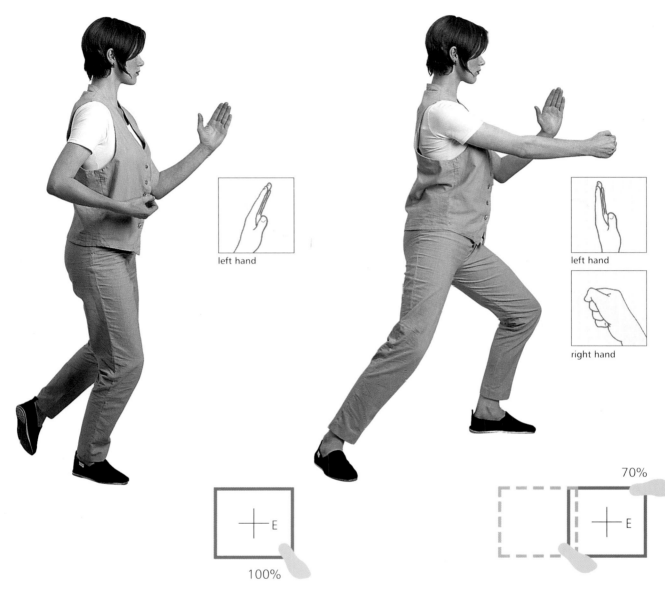

left hand

left hand

right hand

100%

70%

153 *Breathe In*
Prepare to step out to the east by drawing your left toes in just a little toward your right heel. Allow your waist to turn a little in a clockwise direction as you go and draw back the fist in your right hand, knuckles still facing downward, ready to punch. At the same time your left forearm starts to rise, ready to parry. Make sure that there is plenty of space between your right elbow and your side and that your right shoulder remains open and relaxed.

154 *Breathe Out*
Step straight ahead with your left foot, heel first (the third step). As you do this, parry with your left forearm – that is, sweep out with it toward the north from the center. Then, as your left knee bends and as your weight goes forward, punch to the east very slowly – the punch should be central and about solar-plexus height. As your fist goes forward it does a half-turn in midflight, to finish with the thumb side uppermost. Finally adjust the back heel to a comfortable position if necessary.

Release Arm and Push

The Release Arm and Push routine that comes next is identical to that shown at the end of Section Three (see page 41). Remember, keep the rhythm steady throughout and make sure that you keep some space between your elbows and your sides as you carry out the movement.

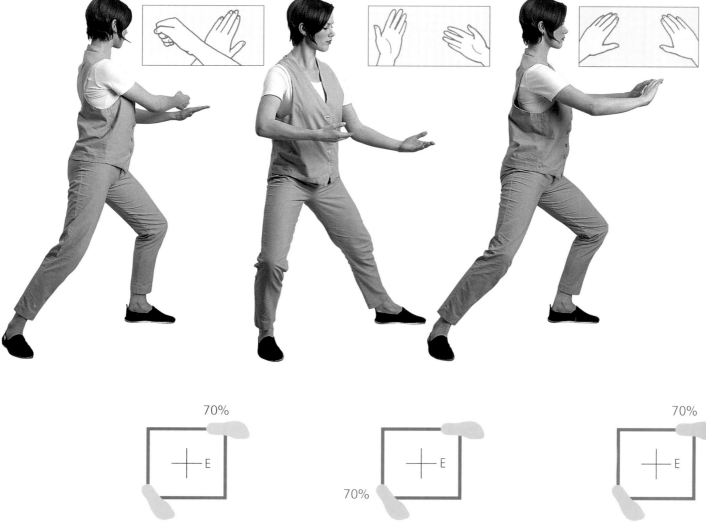

155 *Breathe In*
Begin as before *(see page 41)* by sliding the left hand under the right forearm, turning both palms up and preparing to sit back onto the rear leg. The name – Release Arm – alludes to the martial character of this movement, being a means of releasing the arm from a grip upon the wrist. Do try to cultivate a relaxed and open feeling to the hands and arms throughout.

155a *In-breath Finishes*
The waist now turns slightly clockwise as you bring the weight back into the right leg. Simultaneously you draw the right hand back with the left hand following just a moment later, coming back near to your center where you rotate both wrists in preparation for the push. Again make sure that the front knee does not lock. The front leg should remain soft, with a slight bend to the knee.

156 *Breathe Out*
Next comes the push to the east, made, as always, largely through the actions of the legs, not the arms or shoulders. The shoulders remain relaxed throughout, allowing the chi to flow into the arms and hands. And remember, the weight goes slowly forward, transferring gradually from the right leg to the left leg. Make sure you do not lean forward into the push.

Turn and Cross Hands

Again this routine was first shown at the end of Section Three (see page 42) and occurs once more here to seal in the energies at the end of the entire form. This time, however, the weight remains equally distributed in both feet, and the hands are lowered equidistantly to the sides.

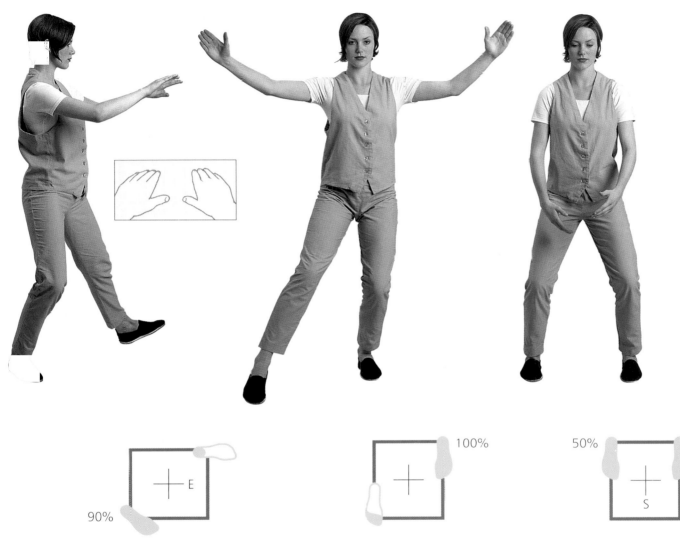

90%   100%   50%

157 *Breathe In* The last movement of the form begins with a weight-shift to the back leg and a certain relaxing down of the hands after the push. The shape formed by the hands is very yin-like in character, with the energy returning inward rather than pushing out as it was a moment ago. In fact, the whole energy of the body can be altered from yin to yang and back again with subtle movements at the wrist.

158 *Breathe Out* Pivot on your left heel to get the toes as near south-facing as you can. The weight then drifts back across to the left side enabling you to raise the right foot and draw it back toward you to create the parallel-feet stance with which we finish the form. You can raise your toes or your heel first to draw back your foot – some people even trail the toes back along the ground. Do not lift the hands higher as you turn.

158a *Out-breath Finishes* Your waist having now rotated to face south, and your feet having reached their parallel position, shoulder-width apart, let your hands complete their generous, circular sweep around and down to the level of the abdomen. The weight now begins to settle evenly in the feet – a rare condition in tai chi, and one that mirrors the situation just after the start of the whole form *(see page 22).*

99

Turn and Cross Hands (continued)

Beginners often encounter difficulty in finishing this movement with the feet in the correct position – that is, shoulder-width apart, parallel and pointing south, as shown below. The trick is to turn in the left foot as much as possible at the start (see step 158 on the previous page) – then it's easy!

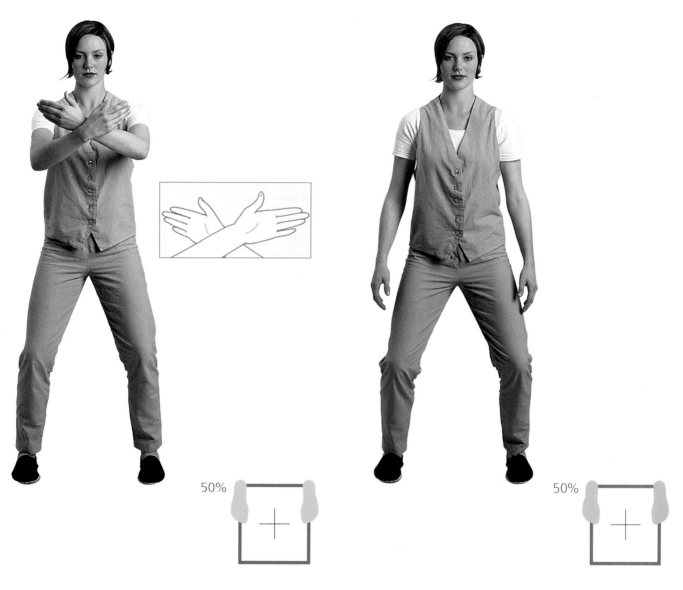

50%

50%

159 *Breathe In*
Raise your hands through the centerline of your body, to about chin-height. Here the wrists cross, left over right – that is, with the left hand closer to your body than the right and with the hands themselves fairly flattened in shape. As always when the hands rise up, make sure the shoulders remain relaxed. Do not lose the subtle bend in the knees, either, and keep your back straight – your body perfectly aligned and balanced.

160 *Breathe Out*
Finally, to conclude the whole of the tai chi form, breathe out and slowly lower both hands down through your center and out to your sides. Let the weight sink down as you go; bend your knees and feel the powerful contact with the earth as the body settles into a well-rooted and yet perfectly relaxed position. Keep a little space under the arms and relax the shoulders. Relax the fingers, too. That's it! You did it – congratulations.

Concluding the Form

At the conclusion of your tai chi, always rest for a moment before moving off. Take some deep breaths and try to experience how your body feels. Visualize the energy circulating freely throughout your entire body, nourishing all the vital organs and systems, and recognize that this energy is somehow a universal substance that flows through everything else around you. This is a time of repose and harmony. Enjoy it!

With practice, you will find that each time you come to the end of the form you will have returned to the same place as you began – your feet finishing on the very same piece of ground that they occupied at the start. This is an interesting feature of the short yang form, wholly practical and useful if you are working within a limited space, but also suggesting a certain cyclical character to the whole exercise.

The Chinese philosophy of life known as Taoism, which we will be looking at much more closely in the second part of this book, has always viewed the process of time as being cyclical rather than linear in nature. In other words, things move in cycles: day follows night and returns to night again; summer follows winter and returns to winter, and so on. It is this natural law (confirmed by modern statistical research, by the way, which has isolated literally thousands of cycles in nature and economic and political affairs) that underpins the notion of the tai chi form as a kind of journey, going forward and taking us forward, too, and yet also always returning to its source.

If there is time available in your daily tai chi routine for a little reflection, then these moments immediately after the conclusion of the form can be a period of considerable illumination.

For when we find ourselves at the end of the form, we have, in a sense, returned from a journey. Along with the many obstacles and challenges encountered and overcome, we have each, in our own way, touched upon the great energies of nature, including several of its most powerful and mysterious creatures. The tai chi form fills our inner senses with images of tigers and cranes, populates it with snakes, horses and birds, with glimpses of strutting pheasants and mischievous monkeys. These splendid, illusive creatures, possessing such calm, dignified strength, as all wild creatures inevitably do in their natural state of health and vigor, are emulated not only outwardly in form as we progress through the movements, but also inwardly, in spirit and instinct, every time we bring them to life.

Working in a perfectly unself-conscious, unmindful way, we should contemplate this inner vision as we go through our steps. Evoke the character of the creatures encountered on the journey and see what they can teach about being at one with the world – perfectly composed, without awkwardness, without fear of what might be, but instead living only in the ever-present "now." Tai chi is a journey of self-discovery – an inspiration to the spirit. That experience can never pale if it is approached in this way. No matter how often repeated, it will always have something fresh to teach us, awakening a deeper understanding each time that we embark upon its mysteries. And it is to the exploration of these exciting inner dimensions of the tai chi experience – the health, spirit and mind of tai chi – that the rest of this book is devoted.

PART TWO

Taking It Further

*P*art Two explores the extra dimensions to tai chi, which normally become apparent after the first few weeks of practice. As the body and mind become harmonized through daily exposure to tai chi we naturally begin to experience the benefits, first in terms of health and then in a mental and emotional context as well. So here we will be looking in more detail at the health benefits that daily practice can bring and also drawing upon the eternal principles of Taoism, locating the pathways of thought along which tai chi can point us – the yang and the yin, the five elements of oriental culture and medicine, and the great path or way that is the eternal Tao itself.

This is not to say that the physical aspect starts to take a backseat. On the contrary, it continues at the center of the learning process, since almost everything that occurs on the mental plane will have its counterpart in the practice of the tai chi form itself. In addition to this, there is a whole area of tai chi study that involves working with others – partner work – an especially stimulating and enjoyable facet of tai chi that is also explored in the following pages.

NINE

Tai Chi and Health

When we begin life we are naturally flexible; as children we are upright and balanced. As we grow older, however, tensions affect the body: joints become tight, the spine loses its mobility and the circulation of blood and vital fluids becomes restricted through muscular tension. Tai chi works against these trends; it is of vast benefit to our overall health and is an excellent form of preventive medicine.

A Healthy Lifestyle

That daily practice of tai chi is good for us is beyond dispute. Even if the numerous statistical studies done in both China and the West are set aside, anyone who has ever done tai chi over any length of time will know how well they feel because of it. So how does it work? How can the simple practice of performing a set of slow-motion movements contribute so significantly to our health and well-being?

Consider the nature of tai chi movement: you work slowly and calmly with the spine upright, encouraging the neck to "sit" in the correct position and reduce tension. Gradually, with the knees slightly bent, your body weight shifts to and fro, the leg muscles working to help pump blood up to the heart. The arms and shoulders are in constant motion, opening and closing in graceful rotational movements, helping to stimulate the lymphatic system and improve lung capacity. You maintain the central equilibrium around the area of the *Tan Tien* – the point just beneath the navel where so much of our natural energy is gathered *(see page 16)*. The concentration and mental focus that this entails produce clarity and stability; your breathing is relaxed and constant, your metabolic rate increases, and your digestive process improves.

With the upright posture there is room for the internal organs to "breathe" and function properly. Air and vital fluids circulate freely, and the mind becomes clearer – refreshed and able to soar, contemplating the great universal forces of ebb and flow, light and shade. And you realize that if you can be centered and happy like this in your body, you can apply this newfound belief in yourself to everything else that you do.

On the next pages, a number of tai chi movements are discussed with regard to how they relate to areas and vital functions of the body. Bear in mind, however, that although some movements within the form are considered to be especially helpful for particular complaints, the strength of tai chi in health terms is found in its overall effect. In other words, in contrast to a therapy such as acupuncture which can target a particular illness, tai chi strengthens the immune system as a whole and so assists the body in finding its own natural level of well-being – a state in which illness is no longer able to thrive or gain a foothold so easily.

In oriental medicine, diagnosis and treatment of illness are built around an energy-based theory rather than a viral/bacterial one, as in the West. 'Chi" is the basis of all physiological processes, and a blockage or disturbance to the flow of chi depriving the vital organs of their natural power source is considered paramount in the process of disease. To understand this process, we need to understand the nature of chi itself, the vital energy of the universe that flows through all things and is responsible for the life within us all, at every moment.

EFFECTS OF TAI CHI PRACTICE

The benefits of practicing tai chi are far-reaching, and you will feel the effects in everything that you do, from simply going about your daily routine to playing sports in which coordination and balance play an integral role. For example:

• **At work**. *Those who practice tai chi find that they are more relaxed and in control of situations that arise during the course of the day, and are also more open to the creative process, since the flow of mental energy is not inhibited by tension. In addition, negative energies in others can be anticipated and dealt with successfully.*

• **Coping with pain**. *If you suffer from chronic arthritis or back pain, the gentle flowing movements of tai chi can help to control and ease your condition, and thereby improve your quality of life.*

• **Skiing**. *Tai chi's emphasis on balance, soft knees and a low center of gravity is of enormous benefit to those learning to ski. The body feels more grounded, more in control. Also, the limbs become better coordinated, and the joints more supple and less prone to injury.*

• **Horseback riding**. *A horse needs a balanced rider to be able to perform what is asked of it. Tai chi allows us to explore self-awareness and develop balance and sensitivity; once these qualities have been developed on the ground, they can then be transferred to the saddle, enabling the rider to transmit clearer signals to the horse.*

Tai Chi Movements and Their Benefits

Here you can see an overview of the benefits associated with some of the individual movements in the tai chi form. A number of these movements can exert a specific influence on certain parts of the body, or can affect some of the systems in our body in a particularly beneficial way.

The Chorus movements such as Separate Hands and Push and Grasp the Bird's Tail are particularly helpful for strengthening the energies of the lungs.

Relaxed rotations of the wrist such as those found in Release Arm and Push have very positive implications for the health of these joints and the numerous nerves and blood vessels that pass through them.

Single Whip and the squatting version of this movement, Snake Creeps Down, can benefit the liver and gallbladder by relieving any stagnation of energy or blood that can occur in these organs.

The emphasis on weight distribution constantly flowing from leg to leg is very helpful in providing load-bearing exercise for the legs and can help delay the onset of diseases such as osteoporosis in the elderly. Golden Pheasant is an obvious example.

Crane Spreads Its Wings is said to benefit the spine and the central nervous system via the gentle stretching and twisting it creates in the spinal column.

All the heel stances and heel kicks are helpful for stimulating the circulatory system, especially the return flow of venous blood to the heart from the lower extremities.

The gentle turning movements of Wave Hands Like Clouds are legendary for their benefits to the digestive system and to the stomach in particular, allowing the stomach to settle its energies and become calm.

The gradual twisting and rotating movements of Four Corners help to disperse stagnation in the hips and also throughout the urinary/ reproductive system.

Repulse Monkey and other expansive movements of the shoulders greatly help in the circulation of lymphatic fluid around the body, essential for dealing with toxins in the body.

MENTAL BENEFITS

Regular practice of tai chi will also help to:
- *Calm your thoughts and steady your mind.*
- *Release your inner creativity.*
- *Increase your levels of concentration.*
- *Help you to deal with stress more easily.*
- *Enable you to resolve problems and conflicts.*
- *Encourage you to let go of unwanted mental baggage.*
- *Open your mind to fresh ideas and opportunities.*

In fairness, it must be stressed that it is far from easy to draw upon concrete scientific evidence for many of the correlations shown here. To set up a scientific experiment, for example, to prove that Crane Spreads Its Wings is beneficial for the central nervous system would be difficult, to say the least, as so many variables would be involved. As stated previously, tai chi's greatest strength lies in its overall effect on the body's health. If you are already unwell, it is always best to seek professional advice and proper medical assistance rather than trying to use tai chi to get yourself out of trouble. For convalescence, however, and in combination with medical treatment, tai chi is excellent, and should always be considered as a means to aid and help speed your recovery.

The Nature of Chi

The chi, or vital energy, within our bodies comes from three sources:

- *Inherited Essence*
- *Food*
- *Air*

First there is the natural energy we are born with – our genetic inheritance. The Chinese, even thousands of years ago, were aware of such a phenomenon, and they called it *Jing*, the "essence" of the individual. The Jing can vary greatly from person to person: we have all met people who, despite all kinds of self-inflicted abuse – smoking, drinking, lack of exercise and so on – are somehow still blessed with astonishing levels of strength and vitality. A supreme example of powerful Jing can be seen in the case of a venerable old French woman who celebrated her 120th birthday. When asked for the secret of her longevity, she suggested that it might have been due to giving up smoking at the age of 104. In fact, this longevity is more than likely due to the Jing she inherited at birth, which ensured that she still had a fine sense of humor, even 120 years later!

The Jing relies not only on the strength of the parents, but also on the health of the mother during pregnancy. Western scientific research bears this out. A study done in Holland showed, for example, that children whose mothers carried them through food shortages during the Second World War became significantly more likely to suffer heart disease in later life than those not exposed in a similar way.

We cannot do anything to alter this initial start in life – rather like being dealt a hand of cards: whether good or bad, we must simply make the most of it. Jing is a fairly finite substance, too, which gradually diminishes as we grow older. However, it's not all bad news! We can preserve what we have by following a reasonably moderate lifestyle, by eating well and by strengthening ourselves through practices such as tai chi or yoga, which exert a favorable influence upon the Jing itself.

Chi also comes from food and air, both of which need to be of good quality if the chi is to be strong. For example, our food needs to be fresh and wholesome, without too many additives; the same goes for the air that we breathe, which should, ideally, be relatively unpolluted and fresh. Chi is more abundant in fresh food and clean air and can be absorbed naturally through the digestive system and the lungs. When combined with the Jing, these natural energy sources give rise to the internal vitality of the body, which maintains and powers all of our physiological functions.

It may help to think of this in mechanical terms. The food can be compared to the fuel we put in our car engines, which has to be mixed with air to be of use. This occurs in the body, too – the air, in this case, coming via the

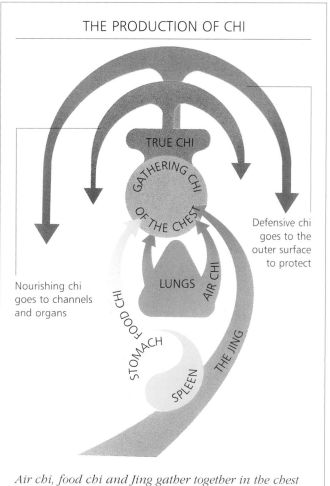

THE PRODUCTION OF CHI

Air chi, food chi and Jing gather together in the chest to form "true chi," in an area known as the Sea of Chi. This chi is then able to nourish and protect the body.

108

lungs. Finally, when the fuel and air are combined, a spark is needed to ignite the mixture and so drive the motor. This is the Jing. The Jing can be likened to the spark plugs in the engine. Tai chi, with its emphasis on breathing and movement from the chest and from the center of the body, helps to build and distribute the vital energy by strengthening the function of the stomach, the spleen and the lungs, those organs most responsible for receiving and processing the external chi of food and air.

The combination of air, food and Jing is considered to be a particularly powerful kind of chi which is formed in the chest area – a place called the Sea of Chi *(see diagram, page 108)*. Once this potent mixture is activated it functions in two distinct ways, first to nourish and then to protect – each of which is essential for maintaining our health and well-being.

The Nourishing Chi

The chi that circulates to the organs of the body is called the nourishing chi. This flows along specific channels called "meridians" – energy lines that are worked in therapies such as shiatsu, and along which most of the acupuncture points of oriental medicine are located *(see right)*. Most of these channels flow deep into the body and into the vital organs, from which they take their names – for example, we have the Spleen channel, the Liver channel and so on (in oriental medicine, the organs are written with a capital letter to reflect their role as a "sphere of function," rather than merely a physical structure).

The organs and their channels, moreover, do not function in isolation, but are known to constantly feed energy to each other in endless cycles of mutual support and control. This interdependence is traditionally represented by the five elements of oriental medicine: Water, Fire, Metal, Wood and Earth. The Kidneys relate to the Water element, the Heart to Fire, the Lungs to Metal, the Liver to Wood and the Spleen to Earth. The illustration on the next page shows this mutual dependence: you can see, for example, that the Kidney energy helps to support the Liver, the Liver energy helps to support the Heart and so on *(see also pages 129–133)*.

THE MERIDIANS

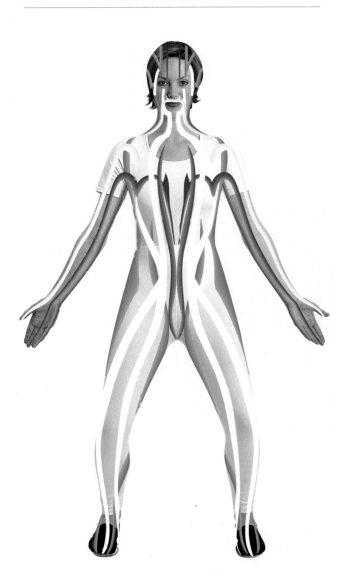

KEY TO MERIDIANS

FIRE	▬▬▬	Heart (and Pericardium) and Small Intestine
WOCD	▬▬▬	Liver and Gallbladder
WATER	▬▬▬	Kidney and Bladder
METAL		Lung and Large Intestine
EARTH		Stomach and Spleen

Here you can see the major meridians of the body along which the nourishing chi circulates. Each of these meridians is associated with a pair of organs and one of the five elements, according to oriental medicine (see above key).

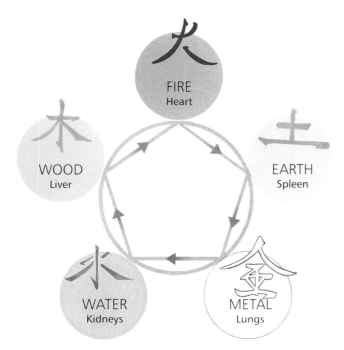

The five elements of oriental medicine function in a mutually dependent state, feeding energy to each other in a continual cycle of support.

Our emotions can upset our internal balance in a big way. Anger, sorrow, shock, fear – all these can upset the organs, eventually producing physical tension and, ultimately, illness. For example, fear injures the Kidneys and this in turn affects the back, whereas sadness damages the Lungs and therefore has an effect on the chest. The typical relaxed and balanced attitude cultivated by regular tai chi practice helps to channel harmful emotions safely. The typical tai chi mind is cheerful, open, optimistic and philosophical, and not given to anger, greed, confrontation or excessive pride. It is, therefore, able to ride the tide of modern living, with all of its illusory values, and so maintain a state of inner harmony and balance.

The Protective Chi: The Body's Defensive Shield

Apart from the existence of chi as vital energy within the channels and organs, it also circulates nearer to the surface of the body where it performs another very special task. This kind of chi is related to the immune system of the body, and the Chinese see it as being rather like a defensive shield protecting us from external pathogens. They call it the protective chi.

The Lungs play an important part in the distribution of this particular form of vital energy;

indeed, whenever we succumb to illness it often takes the form of a respiratory disease first, such as a sore throat, runny nose, and coughs and sneezes. This is the body's defense system, the protective chi, trying to combat the invading pathological factor and destroy it.

If our levels of defensive chi are strong, the invading pathogens will be fought off successfully, but if not, it is likely that a more chronic illness will develop. Tai chi cultivates this protective chi and strengthens the defensive shield, and those who practice regularly will rarely suffer from colds or flu. This is a good sign indicating that the immune system itself is in good shape and working away to keep the body fit and well at all levels, inside and out.

EVIDENCE FOR THE EXISTENCE OF CHI

A number of successful research experiments into the effects of chi within the body have been conducted in the West, but the medical establishment is generally unaware of the vast number of studies that have also been carried out in China, many of which have remained virtually unknown outside of that country. Here are some examples of what has been found, in both the East and the West. These results go some considerable way toward proving not only that chi exists, but also that there are discernible physiological differences associated with the meridians and acupuncture points, supporting the traditional oriental view that chi flows throughout all of the body.

• *Scientists in Beijing have examined human tissue to check the thickness of the layers of cells making up the skin. In most of the samples, the layer of skin was found to be thinner along the traditional acupuncture meridian lines.*

• *Those searching for the effects of chi on the structure of the nervous system have discovered a difference in the structure of nerves on meridian lines as compared with surrounding areas.*

• *It has long been known that the electrical resistance of the skin at the location of acupuncture points is lower than elsewhere on the body.*

• *At Harvard University experiments have been conducted on reducing high blood pressure by chi kung therapy – the transmission of chi from one person to another via touch. Treatment with chi kung therapy consistently produced results superior to conventional hypertension drugs.*

Quality of Movement

So what exactly causes things to go wrong? What are the factors that damage or inhibit the flow of chi in the body? Emotional pressures, lifestyle, poor diet and a general lack of rapport with the natural environment are all important influences. Also, the natural harmony between the internal family of organs can be upset by injury to the organs or even to the tissues, bones and muscles through which their channels flow. Conversely, tension, bad posture or habitually awkward movements affecting the channels can eventually be transferred back to the organs themselves.

For instance those who work for long periods slumped over a desk or keyboard often develop a stagnation or deficiency of energy in the chest area, thereby weakening the Lungs and making them susceptible to common respiratory diseases such as colds or flu. Those who stand for long periods may suffer from hip and back pain, again due to long-term congestion of energy in those areas and within the Kidneys as well. The repetitive strain of our daily working routine can place great demands on our health. Correct alignment of the body is essential, therefore, for the smooth flow of chi. Such alignment is a fundamental principle of tai chi practice.

It is for this reason that other forms of exercise fall short of tai chi in terms of lasting results. Studies clearly show, for example, that tai chi is more effective than aerobics in reducing high blood pressure. In other words, it is the nontensile quality of movement, rather than the quantity of repetitions, that counts in any given exercise session. And that is also why – for all its promise and rich potential – tai chi's benefits will only ever accrue if the movements themselves express this precise quality of relaxation and calm. To this end, once you have learned the mechanics of the form from Part One, you can start to focus on certain refinements.

Begin by trying to be aware of what is going on in your body – for instance, really learning to relax those arms! Saying it is one thing, but achieving it is quite another. Always visualize the tension and tightness of the muscles and sinews melting away and dissolving as you work. This allows the chi to flow through the arms and hands. The importance of this principle cannot be overemphasized. Drop your shoulders! Let your hands float! Remind yourself to do this constantly, every day and every time you practice tai chi, and your movements will soon become smooth and graceful.

However, do not forget that the pursuit of gracefulness is not an end in itself. If taken to extremes, it can result in your tai chi becoming weak and monotonous, without any kind of energy at all. At its best, tai chi combines relaxation with movement – and this is what creates the energy. Stillness with tension, on the other hand, merely produces stagnation; and the form should never be done so slowly or ponderously that it leads to this kind of malaise.

With this in mind, it is essential that you *keep moving*. A common error among beginners is to pause or even in some cases to pose at the conclusion of each movement. This kind of tai chi often goes with an irregular, stop-start kind of rhythm in which individual movements are rushed, only to result in a "lifeless" pause at the finish of each one. Make sure you do not become a poser! Keep the movements gradual, smooth and, above all, fluent – like a floating cloud or a running stream, always in motion.

POINTS TO REMEMBER

To get the most out of your tai chi practice and to let your chi flow smoothly and freely, pay attention to the following reminders:

- *Always visualize the tensions of the body dissolving as you work.*
- *Drop your shoulders, bend your knees and keep your spine straight.*
- *Always maintain some energy in your limbs – never go limp.*
- *Keep moving at all times - do not pose.*
- *Make sure your hips are level.*
- *Keep your rate of breathing slow and rhythmic, but never forced.*

Quality of Life

Unfortunately, for all its benefits, tai chi is not a universal remedy. There are always other factors that need to be taken into account if you are going to give the exercises a fair chance to do their best for you. Most of these are related to lifestyle and things that can be easily controlled. A few are listed here for your consideration.

Extremes of Climate

Illness can often be aggravated or even directly caused by extremes of climate. Cold, heat and damp are climates that we recognize as having the potential to affect our health, yet it is surprising how many of us ignore common sense and expose ourselves to the effects of these conditions. For instance going outside with wet hair on a cold day or failing to protect your head from direct sunlight on a hot day are common errors which can bring about illness even months after the event. These are things that most of us do without giving it a second thought.

Wind can also cause illness, which may come as a surprise to some. The Chinese say that wind is the spearhead of disease, as it is often combined with cold or heat and opens up the body to external pathogens. Excessively dry conditions can also be damaging. Above all, make sure that you protect your body from extremes of climate and dress according to the seasons. Areas that need special protection in winter, for instance, are the head, throat, kidneys and ankles.

EFFECTS OF CLIMATE

According to oriental medicine, different climatic conditions affect different areas of the body:
- *Heat damages the Heart.*
- *Damp damages the Spleen.*
- *Dryness damages the Lungs.*
- *Cold damages the Kidneys.*
- *Wind penetrates the body's defenses and affects the Lungs and the Liver.*

Diet

Diet is very important. No matter how conscientiously you work at the tai chi form, without a good foundation of food to nourish the body, your health will certainly suffer. Food should be wholesome and warming, so avoid junk food and foods that are heavy and full of saturated fats and sugars. Beware also of food fads and "wonder" diets. Keep in mind the teachings of oriental medicine, based on thousands of years of experience of how the human body works.

Too much raw, cold food, for example, is considered to be highly detrimental. It can damage the digestive process, particularly if consumed during cold weather. Generally speaking, food should be cooked or heated in some way, especially if you live in a cold climate. Above all, always eat a good substantial breakfast to warm the stomach, otherwise it will not be able to provide the body with adequate chi.

Mental Health

Try to keep your mind clear of worry. Worry injures the digestive system, while fear and sadness injure the Kidneys and Lungs respectively. Stress injures the Heart, and psychological stress can also affect the body's self-healing mechanism. Numerous scientific experiments have demonstrated a link between healing and stress – the two being mutually exclusive. Of course, there are times when we are forced to cope with stressful situations; stress can even be stimulating in certain circumstances. However, long-term exposure certainly has a debilitating effect on our health, so try to keep your levels of stress down to a minimum.

Negative Thought Patterns

Remove negative thought patterns, in particular anger. Anger is of no use to anyone; it saps the energy of the body on all levels and leads to disease, especially of the Liver and Gallbladder. Some people make an occupation of being angry with things – this is of no benefit to themselves or others. You need to let go of anger instead of bearing a grudge against those who have angered or injured you in the past. An inability to let go of the past is also a form of illness – and only you can heal yourself of this.

Your Body's Needs

Seek medical attention when necessary and use complementary therapies even when you are well. Explore the wide range of therapies available: acupuncture, shiatsu, reflexology, homeopathy, aromatherapy, to name but a few. There are many to choose from. Find one that suits you and visit a practitioner regularly as a preventive measure to ward off illness before it arises.

Use your powers of anticipation and judgment to comprehend your own health process.

Tai chi puts you in touch with your body's needs; listen to your body and act accordingly. It is a wonderful self-regulating and self-healing system. Look after it with kindness and affection and, ultimately, you may even be able to use your powers to help others in times of illness.

Tai Chi: The Healing Touch

When most people touch one another they are usually engaged in one of two typical human pursuits: either making love or fighting. Setting aside the occasional hug to friends or family, the art of touch is something that is much neglected and, in the Western world, almost entirely lost. Yet if we look at other primates and examine their social behavior, we find that touch in the form of grooming is an almost constant activity; in fact, many mammals and birds touch and groom one another as part of their normal, everyday activity.

Those engaged in healing professions such as massage, shiatsu and reflexology are trained to transmit healing energy to their patients via touch. This is an important addition to the application of the therapy itself, without which the work of healing is often void of any great impact.

Touch is a way of exchanging chi – therapist to patient – usually involving the transmission of good chi from the therapist to replace an area where the patient's chi is absent or congested. In shiatsu it is often said that a practitioner has "good hands," which simply means that they can transmit their chi, both mental and physical chi, to others. There is no great trick to this, and most of us can transmit some measure of healing energy when we really want to. But the whole process is greatly facilitated if our own body is free of unnecessary tension.

Tension is the enemy of chi. The chi cannot flow through a body that is constricted with muscular tension or negative mental energy. Many therapists have their own personal regimen of exercise or meditation to combat this, particularly prior to a treatment session. Tai chi is especially suitable for this purpose, as not only does it prepare you mentally for the work, but in the long term it actually allows you to open up to the universal source of chi, which can then flow directly through you to the patient.

This universal chi is in fact not only very powerful and effective, but also absolutely limitless. Only an empty vessel can receive energy, however, which makes it especially important to go "yin" – to become empty and let the chi flow. Tai chi teaches you how to be empty, how to receive – and then, ultimately, how to project and give back. To therapists of all persuasions it really is the ultimate companion to your life's work.

TEN

Partner Work

It is tempting to view tai chi as a relatively solitary pursuit, done for one's own pleasure and satisfaction, but this is not the case. Often people gather together to share their experiences; there are also clubs and schools that teach the form in groups. And there is a whole area of tai chi practice that involves close contact with others; this section offers simple exercises for working with a partner.

Working Together

If you go to classes in tai chi or if you have a friend or partner sharing your interest in the subject, it is possible for you to enjoy a whole set of exercises and routines in which you both work together to develop your skills and enhance your sense of balance and concentration. Exercises of this kind also feature prominently in all tai chi schools where the emphasis is more on the martial arts aspect of tai chi.

They go broadly by the name of Push Hands – an immensely complex area. However, if your interests are more geared toward the health and relaxation aspects of tai chi, there are still a number of simple routines – adapted from traditional techniques – that you can enjoy with a partner and that can be of great benefit to you in your tai chi studies. Four different routines are featured in this section.

BENEFITS OF PARTNER WORK

The Push Hands exercises will help you to do the following:

- *Become more aware of your personal space.*
- *Develop an understanding of the energies of yin and yang.*
- *Enhance your sense of touch and receptivity.*
- *Promote greater balance and stability in your stance.*
- *Sharpen your coordination and qualities of anticipation.*
- *Remove tension from the arms and shoulders.*
- *Learn to govern aggression, impatience and other fundamental weaknesses.*
- *Cultivate intuition and self-confidence.*

Following

The first piece of partner work we are going to look at – Following – uses the movements of your partner as a mirror through which any flaws in your own physical condition can be revealed. For instance, there could be areas of tension or deficiency that you may not have been aware of before. Once you recognize the problem, you can deal with it: you may need to correct your stance to improve your balance, for example, or perhaps to relax the muscles that are causing the tension in your body, and so on.

Below. *Prepare by standing facing each other, not too far apart, with one foot (it does not matter which one) slightly forward. For every follower there must be a leader, so decide now, before you begin, on who will be leading and who will be following. To start with, the leader's job is simply to hold out her hands and allow the follower to place his hands lightly on top.*

Right. *The leader then moves her hands very slowly and at random, in the typical slow tai chi rhythm – up and down, side to side – anywhere that seems appropriate. All the while, the follower tries to keep in touch with the leader's hands, without exerting any kind of grip or pressure. In fact, you will find that the more relaxed you can make your hands and arms, the easier it will be for you to stay in contact. Once you feel confident, try to introduce some subtle body movement – bend the knees, turn the waist a little or, eventually, take the odd step or two. But be sparing with the footwork, or you may lose the sense of calm.*

LOOKING INWARD

As you can see from these illustrations, both partners have their eyes closed during this exercise. This helps to develop the intuitive faculties and also encourages us to use the sense of touch more efficiently. You may not want to work with your eyes closed the very first time you do this routine, but thereafter do try to close them. You will soon get used to it, and if you lose touch at any time, just open your eyes and start again. There is no contest, no element of competition here. The leader's job is merely to make the movements as interesting as possible, with plenty of variety. You are not trying to lose your partner by being clever, or to gain an advantage through force. Just enjoy it and share the experience in a spirit of harmony and trust. And remember, while you are working try to identify problem areas – is there tension in your shoulders, hips, knees or hands, for example? Look inward and become aware.

Above. *Continue in this way for a couple of minutes, or for as long as the leader feels it is appropriate, at which point the leader signals to the follower that this part of the routine is at an end. This is done by simply bringing the palms together. This is an unambiguous signal to the follower that the first half of the routine is complete. Then you simply reverse roles.*

Right. *The leader now becomes the follower and the follower becomes the leader. Begin the exercise once more and continue until, again, the leader feels that the session is ready to come to an end and signals to the partner by bringing the hands slowly together to finish. That completes the whole sequence. It can be repeated as often as you like, and if there is a group of you, you can go on to change partners, too.*

Two-handed Pushing

This exercise helps enormously in learning to stand and move correctly with a good amount of space between the feet. Unlike in the previous exercise, the eyes are open throughout, and there is also a slight element of assertiveness involved, since you are each trying, in a very subtle and nonforceful way, to expose the other's weaknesses. At the same time, you respond to the changes brought about by your partner's body movement and use this to develop an inner, sixth sense as to what is about to happen next.

Left. Begin by facing each other and place one foot forward. Your partner should place the same foot forward as you – in this instance, it is the left foot. Hold out your palms and make light contact as shown here.

Above. Then it is simply a case of one of you pushing gently and slowly forward by bending the knee, while the other retreats and sits back on the rear leg. The other then returns the push, and so on, back and forth. After a while it becomes clear that a good wide stance enables you to react and absorb the push more effectively. In fact, when you are pushed try to respond at the same speed, so that your partner does not feel resistance. If your partner pushes slowly, you retreat slowly, maintaining contact; if your partner pushes quickly, you retreat more quickly, still maintaining light contact between the palms.

Right. *The next stage of this exercise is for one of you to step back as you are pushed, just one pace behind. If your partner is daydreaming and not concentrating he or she will lose contact with your hands and you will, in a sense, have won a little victory. Ideally, however, your partner will be able to respond to your movements and will step forward as you step back, thereby maintaining contact the whole time.*

Below left. *Here, the step has been made successfully, and hand contact has been maintained. It is important here not to get too carried away with the idea of stepping. Again, as with the previous exercise, be sparing with this kind of maneuver, otherwise a certain chaos will inevitably ensue and neither of you will have much time to listen to the movements and sensations within your own bodies, which is precisely what this exercise is designed to achieve.*

Below. *Either one of you can step back in this way and test the other's powers of concentration and intuition. Then you can try stepping forward, as if closing in with your push. Again your partner should be alive enough to your movements to respond in kind by stepping back, as shown here. Thereafter, you can continue by either stepping forward or back, whatever you feel is appropriate. However, make sure you only step back when receiving the push, and only step forward when instigating the push yourself. That way both of you will not be stepping back at the same time, and the contact can be maintained throughout.*

119

One-handed Pushing

Although this may sound like a simplified version of the previous exercise, it is in fact far more challenging. This is because once you begin one-handed pushing, it will inevitably introduce rotational movements of the waist.

This pushing and rotation also has to be co-ordinated with certain weight changes in the feet – all of which becomes effortless and perfectly natural once you have practiced for any length of time.

Above. *Begin by facing each other with the same foot forward, as before. Then both raise your right hand and place your palms together. Without moving the feet at all, one person then pushes forward by bending the knee while the other sits back. In the illustration here, for example, you can see that the woman has already pushed against the man's palm, and he has sat back into his rear leg. Note the turn in the waist. You will find that as you sit back, your waist will naturally want to turn to accommodate the movement.*

Right. *As with the previous exercise, you can add interest and variety to this routine by stepping forward or back with the push. When this occurs, however, you will need to change hands. This is best illustrated by a sequence of photographs, beginning here, once again, with both of you having placed your left foot forward, making contact with your right hands.*

Right. *Next, one of you decides to step forward with the right foot. In the illustration here, for example, the man is just about to step ahead with his right foot and push out with his left hand.*

Below. *As the person pushing steps forward, the other should anticipate this move by stepping back while at the same time presenting the other palm to push against. This is the stage that has been reached here; the woman has anticipated his move and, having stepped back with her left foot, has just presented her left palm for him to push against. With practice this anticipation will happen naturally. Always turn at the waist to accommodate the push.*

Below. *Once the step has been taken, you and your partner can return to the simple pushing routine with the feet stationary, only this time the right foot is forward with the left palms in contact. Take it in turns to push forward by alternately bending your knee to bring your weight forward and then sitting back on your rear leg as your partner pushes back, rotating your waist as necessary throughout the exercise.*

OPTIONS

Of course, you can always choose to begin the routine with the other foot forward – it is up to you. The two options are:
• *Both partners have the left foot forward at the start, with the right palms in contact.*
• *Both partners have the right foot forward at the start, with the left palms in contact.*
Do not introduce too many steps during the exercise; you should only step occasionally, whenever you feel that your partner's concentration might be wavering.

Single Push Hands

This is a relatively advanced exercise, since you are urged to alternate between a basic one-handed push and a tai chi-style Ward Off. In other words, you present your forearm for your partner to push against and then push back against his or her forearm directly afterward in the typical seesaw motion already encountered. Only attempt this, therefore, once you feel comfortable with the preceding routines. Cooperation is essential; try to respond to your partner's pressure so his or her efforts do not meet with a sense of opposition.

Left. *Begin, again, by facing each other with the same foot forward (in this case, the left foot). One of you then offers the right wrist and forearm in a Ward Off, similar to that found in the tai chi form (see page 26) while the other pushes forward with the palm of the right hand. This is clearly shown in this photograph, where the woman has begun by offering her right wrist and forearm, and the man is just about to push forward against the back of her wrist with the palm of his right hand.*

Below. *If you are the one receiving the push, sit back on your rear leg and turn your waist slightly to accommodate the movement. By going yin like this – that is, emptying and yielding for a moment – you are able to absorb your partner's yang (pushing) energy and deflect it away to the side. As with the previous exercise, provided the stance is good and wide, your waist is able to turn with great flexibility.*

Right. *Next the hands reverse. Whoever was previously doing the Ward Off now rotates the wrist in order to push back against the partner's wrist, which has itself rotated to a Ward Off position, palm facing in. These rotations should happen simultaneously each time the push is returned, keeping the contact.*

Below. *As soon as the person pushing forward does so, the other retreats in the same way as the partner did a moment ago, turning the waist, becoming yin and thereby absorbing the oncoming yang energy without resistance.*

Below. *After this the hand positions are reversed once more and the whole process can be repeated, back and forth, for as long as you both wish. After a while you can start the routine again with a different foot forward or a different arm raised (see suggestions given below).*

VARIATIONS

Here are some suggestions on how to vary this exercise:
• *Both partners have the left foot forward and the right arm raised (as shown here).*
• *Both partners have the right foot forward and the left arm raised.*
• *Both partners have the left foot forward and the left arm raised.*
• *Both partners have the right foot forward and the right arm raised.*
Always make sure that it is the same foot and the same arm for both of you, otherwise it can get rather messy. Also, you must not become irritable and lose patience, which is very easy to do.

Yielding As Strength

There is a deeper significance to partner work and Push Hands, and in each of the four exercises featured on the previous pages we find the forces and qualities of yang and yin, demonstrated not just on a physical level, but on a mental or internal level as well. Yang is dynamic, thrusting energy; yin is soft, yielding empty space. Both these qualities are of equal value and are just as powerful in their own way. The notion of yielding in order to deal with an oncoming force is an unfamiliar one in Western thought, yet it is has much to commend.

An army without flexibility never wins a battle.
A tree that is unbending is easily broken.

Tao Te Ching

In Taoist philosophy – the way of thinking that underlies tai chi itself – the "life-principle" is equated to the very yin-like qualities of suppleness and flexibility, without which there can be only inertia, stiffness and, ultimately, death. Flexibility means a willingness to adapt, to embrace the qualities of originality and versatility. In a social situation, for instance, without compromise and a willingness to listen to other people's ideas, progress of any kind is often severely limited and little can be learned from others. A human being is a vessel of a kind, and if the vessel is always full and constantly resisting the currents trying to flow into it from the outside world, nothing of value will ever have room to enter; this results in mental stagnation, in which opportunities for change and evolution are simply missed.

All these ideas are given physical form in the Push Hands exercises, where we learn to relax and let go and not to be disturbed or unbalanced by the energies coming in our direction. Rather, we ride these energies, turn them around and use them constructively, without becoming aggressive and without becoming angry.

More than anything, partner work of this kind cultivates patience. It eliminates, in time, the illusory distinctions between victory and defeat, winning and losing. In this sense, the more you can yield, the greater your strength; the more you give, the greater your abundance. In partner work, your emotions should remain constant during your practice – even and unruffled throughout, full of kindness and regard for your partner. Never forget that you are also observing your own actions as you work. It really does not matter how often your faults are exposed, nor how often you are off-balanced or lose contact, because each time this occurs you can learn something about yourself.

In Push Hands, as in all of life, being made aware of our faults through our interaction with others is no disgrace, but rather a gift that can help us to change and evolve. The sign of a good Push Hands session is that laughter and happiness can always be seen in the faces of

Remember, there's no contest. Enjoy it!

124

those taking part. When this spirit of enjoyment is lacking, however, there is merely bewilderment, or a somewhat feverish preoccupation with pride and the desire to defeat another person at some illusory contest. This, of course, is not the spirit of tai chi. With Push Hands, as soon as you feel the least bit irritable, as soon as you sense the slightest gesture of retaliation in yourself, you have already been defeated, overcome by your own egoism. If this happens, you must simply start again. The lessons of Push Hands are enormous; what you learn will benefit you not just in tai chi practice, but in every aspect of your life.

The Martial Tai Chi

Even in the light of this very brief glance at partner work, it should be apparent that there can be a substantially physical edge to the practice of tai chi. To many of us, inspired by the poetry and graceful beauty of the movements, this may seem something of a paradox, but we must not forget that tai chi is also a martial art.

Since this book focuses on the therapeutic aspects of tai chi, the martial side has only been briefly touched upon in the Introduction. However, it is worth being aware of the fact that every one of the movements included in the form has a martial application, no matter how subtle or how hidden this may seem when the movement is performed. Obviously, in a combat situation the movements themselves are done at speed, and through Push Hands practice, further skills can be developed in which the opponent can be uprooted or thrown, although the exercises included in this book are not intended for this purpose!

The name "tai chi" is actually a shortened, Westernized version of the full name, "Tai Chi Ch'uan," and the distinction between the two terms is not without relevance. "Ch'uan" can be loosely translated as "fist" or "fighting system," or even "control," reflecting tai chi's origins as a martial art around the twelfth century A.D.; indeed, most of the great masters of tai chi over the ages have been adept in this field. The popular shortening of the name, however, reflects the recent surge of interest in the therapeutic quality of tai chi practice, as more and more people turn to it as an ideal "antidote" to today's hectic lifestyle.

In the East, where the health and relaxation benefits of tai chi are enjoyed by vast numbers of people of all ages and levels of fitness and by people from all walks of life, there has never been any problem with these two different approaches, or with any other of life's rich and diverse opinions and contradictions. In oriental medicine, for example, where modern scientific discoveries are able to exist quite happily alongside more traditional diagnostic techniques, a doctor will have no difficulty whatsoever in considering an illness to be, on the one hand, a viral infection leading to acute bronchitis and, on the other, a manifestation of "wind and heat" invading the Lungs.

In its spread to the West, however, where there is a tendency to place things into neat compartments to be labeled as either one thing or another, tai chi's natural diversity has sometimes been questioned. And aspiring students wanting to learn the form can sometimes be disappointed if they go along to tai chi classes only to be told that all their aspirations toward calmness, tranquillity and grace must be set aside – that tai chi is really a martial art and that if they intend to take the subject at all seriously, they should be focusing on sparring and fighting instead.

From a certain perspective this may be true, and the extensive training and discipline required to develop martial skills in tai chi are in themselves laudable. Ultimately, whatever approach is taken will depend upon the interests of the teacher or school involved, and this can vary enormously. But as the flourishing popularity of tai chi continues to knock at the door of Western consciousness, it must be remembered, too, that many of its working principles come from the gentle healing arts of China, and from the timeless philosophy of Taoism. Tai chi is, in fact, a wonderfully diverse subject, with space enough for warriors and poets, fighters and doctors, yang and yin on all levels. And it is therefore to this area – the philosophy of tai chi and the integration of mind, body and spirit – that we turn next.

ELEVEN

The Eternal Cycle

In the West tai chi is often portrayed solely as a form of physical exercise or, as we have just seen, a martial art. We have also explored its relationship with the principles of oriental medicine in the section on health at the beginning of this part of the book. And yet even this view of tai chi falls short of the overall picture, since the subject itself has at its heart a deeply spiritual and ethical core.

The Journey of Tai Chi

In the midst of movement of the kind found in tai chi – that is, calm, cyclical movement – there is always a point of special stillness. It is from this place that our true potential can arise: all the creative energy that is normally only associated with natural forces, to be found in other creatures or sometimes also in the spontaneity of children. Yet the potential within each of us, young or old, is great indeed, and it is from this potential that we can begin to take charge of our lives. With this flowering of our own inner understanding, many of the more negative patterns of modern living can be overcome; and illness, confusion and feelings of vulnerability need no longer trouble us quite so much as they perhaps once did.

For all its wonders and benefits, however, simply concentrating on the physical side of tai chi can actually become detrimental to our well-being in the long run. This is no idle statement. The energies that tai chi releases can be quite formidable at times and, ultimately, destructive if not tempered by wisdom, self-respect and care for the welfare of others. Power in itself is utterly useless unless it is coupled with control which, in human terms, means self-discipline. And this, if it is to be the real thing and not simply some false regimen of self-imposed restraint, can only come from genuine mental and spiritual strength.

Taoism

Long ago, the ancient Chinese culture gave birth to a particularly interesting and, in many respects, wholly modern form of thinking that resulted in the philosophy called Taoism (pronounced "Dowism"), which we have so far only briefly touched upon. It is not generally appreciated how thoroughly the Chinese mind explored, experimented with and investigated so many diverse doctrines and patterns of organizing their society. Over the several thousand years of China's history, all manner of political and social systems came and went, their leaders and politicians working through the whole spectrum of religious and political coloration.

Around the sixth century B.C., however, there came into being a crystalization of ideas of immense sophistication, based on many centuries of human thought and endeavour. This was Taoism, preserved now in its most enduring form in the classic book the *Tao Te Ching*, reputedly written by a scholar named Lao Tsu around this time.

Overcoming others requires force;
Overcoming the self requires strength.

Tao Te Ching

This quotation is especially relevant to those engaged in tai chi practice. It is saying that it is relatively easy to bully, coerce and dominate others, but very difficult to master the pride and pomposity within that makes us want to do so. The strength referred to here is genuine inner strength, something enduring and rare, and a quality much revered by the Taoists.

So what shape and form does this strength take? Principles such as compassion and kindness feature prominently; and, because chi is viewed as a universal life-force that flows through all things, it should be evident that all forms of life, in whatever shape or form, are in a sense of equal value. This should encourage us to respect the lives of other creatures just as much as we value our own process of living. Taoism, therefore, has a wholly modern, ecological slant in which the natural harmony between all living things is recognized and venerated.

Humility is another feature of this kind of strength. Humility is not a very fashionable word; people often equate it with having low self-esteem or no self-confidence, but this is to confuse humility with timidity. Genuine humility is not about groveling and self-abasement, but rather about having the courage to be open to other people's ideas, ideas perhaps greater than those we have cultivated ourselves, as

127

individuals, over the course of our own brief lives. Humility is about the willingness to listen and learn, even though it may threaten our pride. This can ultimately only make us stronger, not weaker.

These thoughts and reflections are typical of those that governed the society in which tai chi ch'uan was born and consequently grew. But there was also another prevailing pattern that arose around the same time, that of the sage and philosopher Confucius.

Confucianism is the doctrine of social discipline and order in which the authority of family and state are placed above the wishes of the individual – a very different sentiment to the spontaneity and freedom prized by the Taoists. But, in fact, what grew out of the parallel existence of these two sets of values was a typical blending of yang and yin to which people could subscribe without difficulty, leading their personal lives according to Taoism, while at the same time understanding the importance of Confucianism as a code of conduct for large numbers of people living together in the society and state.

Sadly, it does not occur to most people in the West that these two seemingly opposing structures can be successfully integrated. In youth, for example, we are often tempted to rebel, to drop out, become anarchic and live without stability or purpose. With the passing of the years we tend, on the other hand, to become more and more conventional, governed by customs and traditions that may, in effect, actually serve to oppress and bind our individuality.

The philosophy underlying the tai chi experience, however, has no room for extremes and instead seeks to reconcile all opposites – not only in a physical sense, but mentally as well. This is the synthesis of yang and yin in our lives: it is a process that can be likened to a journey, traveling toward the source in a spirit of calm and optimism through all the change and diversity of the world around us.

The Path of Life

The Tao is usually translated as "the Way" or "the Path." It is an all-embracing principle of life that, due to the limitations of the human intellect, cannot be described or known through the normal process of thought or observation. The nearest we come to understanding the Tao is through contemplation of the way in which it manifests in the world around us. This is seen most clearly in the phenomenon of yang and yin – the opposing forces and principles that may be observed in all related phenomena within the natural world. It is best represented by the *Tai Chi Tu* symbol, the basis of which is to be found in the ancient Chinese classic the *I Ching*, or *Book of Changes*, parts of which date back to the twelfth century B.C.

Yin and Yang reflect all the forms and characteristics existing in the universe.

I Ching

We have already come to appreciate as part of our tai chi studies that all aspects of the natural world can be seen to have a dual aspect: day and night, heat and cold, upward and downward, advance and retreat, movement and stillness. These phenomena, moreover, are not isolated. They are interconnected and exist in a state of constant change – yin may change into yang under certain circumstances, and yang into yin. Such is the dynamism underlying the cycle of day and night, or the annual cycle of the seasons. This, too, is the significance in the *Tai Chi Tu* of the small dots or seeds situated in each half of the circle, indicating the potential for inter-transformation: yin within yang and yang within yin. This is why everything in the universe is seen as changing, never, ever static. Movement is at the very heart of life, just as it is at the heart and center of the tai chi form.

All this is particularly relevant to us as human beings because, as we have seen, our internal physiology is dependent on the interplay of yang and yin. The body and its functions are seen in terms of mutually supporting forces: the muscles of the body, for example, can be viewed as yang, while the bones that support them are relatively yin. Similarly, chi is yang, blood is yin, and so on. An understanding of these principles enables those working in the field of oriental medicine to maintain the human body in a state of health and balance, to help cure illnesses or imbalances when they occur, and even to prevent such disharmonies from arising in the first place.

It is worth remembering, however, that it is not only the world of medicine that works on an appreciation of yang and yin. There are a number of professions and occupations in which an understanding of this kind, even if only instinctive, is important – if not essential. For instance, a good chef or cook will be aware of the interplay of opposites, the sweet and sour, the "hot" and "cold" of food. Similarly, skilled designers or architects will be able to make use of the forces of thrust and counter-thrust in their designs, and the different appearances and textures of materials set one against the other. The same goes for a talented artist, dancer or musician – all will have an instinctive understanding of the idea of opposing forces within their chosen discipline.

A human being results from the Qi of Heaven (Yang) and Earth (Yin) …
The union of the Qi of Heaven and Earth is called human being.

The Nei Jing
(Ancient medical classic of China)

The Elements

While remaining at the heart of all creative endeavor, yin and yang also become visible when they give rise to the various states of matter known as the five elements – Fire, Earth, Metal, Water and Wood. We have already met with the five elements briefly in the section on tai chi and health, where we saw how the vital organs of the body can be classified and approached in this way. In fact, there is nothing in the whole of the universe that cannot be described using combinations of the five elements. From these all things arise, from the tiniest of microscopic creatures right up to the greatest of galaxies spinning in space.

It is worth bearing in mind that the five elements of oriental philosophy and medicine are not in any sense a primitive version of the modern periodic table (the Western physicist's table of elements). Rather, they have always been, and remain to this day, a vital key to understanding those great abstract forces of nature that exist both within and far beyond the human body, and in which all living things inevitably share. Nowhere is this wonderful relationship so clearly expressed as in the cycle of the seasons. By living in harmony with the seasons – their climates, flavors, colors and moods – we can begin to attune ourselves to the great Tao and come to feel more at one with our environment. This is of enormous benefit to our tai chi studies, as it provides a framework for understanding and reclaiming our place within the world of nature, where the root of tai chi itself is always to be found. Here, then, is a brief guide as to how we, as creative, sentient beings, can tap into this amazing source of power and inspiration.

Spring • Wood

In spring the element of Wood bursts forth. Expansive, thrusting, growing and blossoming in all directions, full of freshness and vigor, this is the season that many would call their favorite. For us it is a time of shaking off the winter blues, for making plans and striding out in search of new horizons; a time when the body naturally wants to stretch and to exercise, to travel and to begin new projects.

The organs within the body that relate to the Wood element are the Liver and the Gallbladder, whose energies run predominantly along the sides of the body and limbs or, in the case of the Liver, partly along the inside of the legs as well (see page 109). Being aware of choice – of "which way to turn?" or "which direction to follow?" – is typical of the questions asked of ourselves in the season of spring. This is a time of creating new structures in our lives, of organization and evolution. Failure to do so can result in feelings of stagnation and frustration – the common sensation of being stuck in a rut. And it is interesting to note that some may say, perhaps rather unkindly, that someone lacking the courage to grow and change is "lily-livered."

The color most associated with the Wood element and springtime is green, and the climate is wind – the traditional rousing wind of ancient mythology and folk legend that wakes and shakes and inspires nature to blossom and grow. Foods that stimulate and cleanse the body are suitable at this time, and in most parts of the world nature provides an abundance of early vegetables and herbs to aid in this process. Each element and its season has its own special flavor. The sour flavor is one that works directly on the Liver itself, and helps to cleanse it and rid the body of toxins.

The Liver is a vital organ, performing literally hundreds of separate functions within the body. When its energy is restricted the supply of blood and chi to the rest of the body is greatly affected, leading to stagnation, fatigue, stiffness and pain. Perhaps more so than any other organ, the Liver is very easily damaged by negative emotions and thoughts. That is why being in harmony with the Wood element at this time is also all about surrendering to natural impulses, of pushing boundaries, evolving and making new commitments.

For the creative person, in tune with the natural world, spring is a time for inspiration, for observation and for taking pleasure in all those things that grow – the bud and the branch, the greenery of open spaces and woodlands. Allow your tai chi to expand also, making the movements particularly open and sweeping, encompassing a good deal of space and lateral movement, encouraging your natural boundaries to push outward both physically and mentally. Create your own personal space with the movements and then imagine this space radiating out from the body. The feelings of chi in the earth and air at this time are often particularly strong, as the sap rises and life returns to the countryside. Try to locate this feeling in your limbs as you go through your form. You may actually feel it rising from the ground as you work.

Summer • Fire

Summer is a season of maturing, when plants and creatures of all kinds, taking advantage of the long days and warm nights, are at their most active and productive. For us, too, it is a time of 'doing', of achieving our goals and fulfilling the plans set out in the spring. The element of summer is Fire, reflecting the brilliance and strength of the sun at the height of its powers.

The organs related to Fire are the Heart and the Small Intestine, which pertain to the circulation of blood and the absorption of nutrients, essential power sources for the demands of the high-performance lifestyle that summer requires. The energies of these organs run along the arms, those limbs most used for embracing and holding (see page 109). The Heart, therefore, is all about emotional as well as physical warmth, about contact with others, of feeding the internal fires of inspiration and pleasure. It is a time, in the animal world, to partake in the buzz and excitement of life at its most intense, when territories are set out and families raised and fed to maturity. It is at this time when we, too, naturally become more gregarious and outward-going, forming new relationships and visiting different places in a spirit of adventure and enthusiasm. This is the season of outdoor pursuits, of sand and sea, travel and adventure.

Summer is the hottest season, and the flavor associated with it is bitter – so we can happily indulge in plenty of cooling, leafy foods and drinks, which are yin in nature and therefore help to balance the excessive yangness of our surroundings. Salads, fruits and juices – things that in winter we should approach only with moderation – are in plentiful supply now, and are ideal energy-boosters, light and easy to absorb. They provide valuable coolness and moisture, and also help to refresh and replenish the internal fluids of the body.

In hot weather it is vital to avoid doing tai chi around the time of midday, which is far too yang to provide any sense of balance. Even in the evening the weather can still be very warm and humid, and so unless you are a particularly early riser, allow your tai chi to slow right down – take your time and explore the yin phase of each movement in full. And do not forget, if you do perspire during tai chi or any other form of exercise, take special care not to become cold afterward. When the pores of the skin are open, as they are with perspiration, the wind can penetrate the body (remember the "spearhead of disease" mentioned on page 112?). Continue to protect the throat and kidneys even in this season of excessive warmth.

Late Summer • Earth

To many, this may seem a strange kind of season, sandwiched in between summer and autumn; and yet in most climates there is a distinct change of tone and character to those days at the end of summer. It is not yet the drying, windy season that heralds the onset of autumn, but rather, although still warm, it is a far more mellow time – a time of harvest and gathering in, a time of enjoying, quite literally, the fruits of our labors. Late summer, and the Earth element with which it is connected, can also be quite a humid period, and the climate most associated with this season is, in fact, dampness.

In the natural world, with the shortening daylight hours, activity is often no less frantic than in the summer, but with a view, now, to building upon experiences and achievements: a time of consolidation. Animals store food at this time – either in the ground or within their own bodies as fat. The organs associated with the Earth element are the Stomach and the Spleen, organs of digestion or – as the Chinese say – of rotting and ripening, transforming and transporting, moving the vital food-chi all around the body to nourish and support us.

The channel energies of the Stomach and the Spleen run along the front of the body and legs (see page 109), and an imbalance in Earth can often result in a lack of emotional stability, being unable to relate in an appropriate manner to one's own needs or to those of others. Sympathy and the ability to think clearly are some of the mental qualities evinced by a strong Earth element. In nature the birds and creatures often gather and flock together during late summer, and for us too it is a time when people naturally congregate, when rural communities enjoy their festivals of the vine and the field; a time of abundance and plenty – and of rejoicing, as well. The flavor of late summer is sweetness, and it is no coincidence that the ripened foods available in such profusion at this time are sweet.

People often like to slow down at this time; and it is perfectly natural to do so after the busy activity of the previous two seasons. Our tai chi can also mellow – and the sight of tai chi figures merging in the early morning mists as they practice outside in parks or gardens is one of the most appealing and enduring images associated with the subject. It is on just such occasions that the forces of yang and yin, light and dark, moisture and dryness, seem to be most balanced and a time therefore to establish those qualities of harmony and peace, stability and calm within ourselves as autumn approaches.

Autumn • Metal

Autumn is the season of change – that word so deeply embedded in the philosophy of Taoism. Change is at the heart of matter according to the Taoists, a constant presence in all things that are alive. When change is absent, there is merely stagnation and death. Autumn, and the element of Metal with which it is associated, is the season when the leaves wither and fall and the seeds are scattered far and wide. It is often also one of the most beautiful times of the year. For us, it can be a time for contemplation and the study of all the varied forms that appear in the natural world, from acorn to pinecone, from mushroom to seed head.

In autumn creatures begin to take cover and start to prepare for the onslaught of winter. It is also a season of contraction and of drying winds – swirling, relentless winds that bite and scour the countryside. The climate associated with autumn is dryness. Grief and sadness are also associated with autumn and the Metal element in oriental philosophy; the color of Metal – white – symbolizes death and mourning. However, this passing away is always viewed as part of a recurring cycle.

The message of autumn, therefore, is not necessarily a gloomy one, but rather one that urges the acceptance of a healthy cleansing, a sweeping away of the old – a process essential for growth and future development. Failure to reconcile ourselves to this fundamental fact of life can result in feelings of isolation and low self-esteem – commonly seen in those whose Metal energies are out of balance.

The flavor of autumn is pungent, and the organs associated with it are the Lungs and the Large Intestine, organs of elimination. It is important at this time of the year, therefore, to take special care of these parts of the body, with cleansing foods that purify and stimulate us internally as well as providing external energy. Ideally, we should start to reintroduce foods that are more warming in character, replacing our summer fruit and salads with cooked meals, taking advantage of the abundance of fresh produce available at this time. Soups and casseroles rich in herbs, spices and mushrooms are some of the more obviously seasonal choices.

The Metal energies flow along the arms and chest, and deep into the abdomen (see page 109). And it is, indeed, the respiratory system that needs to be protected at this time if we are to avoid seasonal ailments such as colds and flu – the deep, abdominal breathing of tai chi being highly beneficial in this sense. With autumn we can naturally allow our body weight to increase, too, as do most creatures faced with winter when hibernation is often the chosen vehicle for survival. And here also we can allow our tai chi movements to contract

a little, to become more "crisp" and concentrated after the free-flowing styles of the warmer seasons. Focus on the breathing process now, and visualize the Lungs and chest bathed in life-giving chi, which extends out at a distance while circulating and nourishing inside. This is the body's protective shield, to see us through the rigors of winter (see also page 110).

Winter • Water

With the short and often overcast days of winter we are compelled to slow down somewhat, and undergo a certain process of retrenchment. Winter relates to the Water element in oriental reckoning, and the organs associated with it are the Kidneys and the Bladder, organs that regulate our internal fluid balance, including our blood pressure. These organs are closely related to emotions such as fear and anxiety. And those expansive, daring urges that were so prevalent in spring and summer are no longer quite as appropriate now. It is natural in winter to seek shelter, to enjoy our home environment, family and friends and to seek the solace and comfort of the hearth or domestic fireside.

Winter also relates to ideas of storage, of living off those achievements that have gone before. The creative mind will focus on the vital element of Water in all its varied forms, from snowflakes to ice, from steam to ocean tides. For above all this is a time of reflection, contemplation, learning from our experiences and reconciling ourselves to a certain natural pause in the flow of things that urges us to rest and renew our energies.

With this in mind, it is unfortunate that many people view winter as some kind of enemy, to be overcome at every available opportunity through holidays in hot, sunny climes, by sunbeds, alcohol, drugs and late nights. Fighting against the natural inclinations that the seasons urge upon us can often upset the body's internal chemistry, and many ailments of this period of the year are brought about by refusing to slow down or to protect and nourish ourselves appropriately.

The flavor associated with Water and the winter season is salt, and this is a time for all manner of rich, warming meals that help us to maintain body weight and energy. Meats and fish can be invaluable foods during the winter season – a time when the body needs a good supply of wholesome dishes. Conversely, winter is a period of the year when cold or uncooked meals can actually cause considerable damage if taken in excess. In winter we need to warm and nourish the yang energies of the body – particularly early in the day. And the simple, though often neglected expedient of a hot breakfast on a winter's morning can help us to ward off all manner of ailments.

Anyone who has ever done tai chi out of doors on a really cold day will realize that the movements of the form will almost inevitably want to speed up after a while. And although certain dynamic breathing techniques can create internal warmth even on the coldest of days, these are quite difficult to master. Instead, we should be prepared for a certain increase in pace and not fret unduly when it occurs. The energies of Water run predominantly along the back of the body and legs *(see page 109)* and they are connected internally to the adrenal glands – so enjoy your kicks and punches at this time. Get those calf muscles working by low, dynamic stances! And why not try a really fast form occasionally in order to stimulate the circulation still further?

Following the Cycle

With winter we have reached the end of our cycle and can look forward to the new year and the birth of spring once again, continuing on our way in tune with the natural elements of the world around us. The eternal cycle of the seasons is, of course, just one of many other cycles – the cycle of the breath, of the day, of the tai chi form, of life and death. Remember that when we view our existence in this way we are experiencing something utterly real, and no one can put a price on such experiences. They are vital to the spirit, and if we can integrate them in no matter how small a way into our daily lives, alongside all the demands and practicalities of modern living, then we will always be able to find the strength we need to evolve and grow.

This, at heart, is the mystical experience of tai chi, combining the five elements within ourselves in a state of health and harmony, contemplating the yang and the yin, the interplay of opposites and all the amazing contradictions of simply being alive until, ultimately – and if we are very fortunate – we might one day arrive at an understanding of the universal Tao itself. It sounds a tall order, difficult to comprehend perhaps. And, of course, its basis is not rooted in rationality, since the Tao is beyond the description of rational language – which is why, for the inquisitive tai chi student in search of meaning beyond the physical form, the question must always remain of "How?" How can we start on the great journey back toward the source? And how can we see it through to any kind of successful conclusion?

In a sense, the answer will be different for each of us, since we all have our own individual Tao, and thus will find the path that is most suitable to ourself. Tai chi is just one such path.

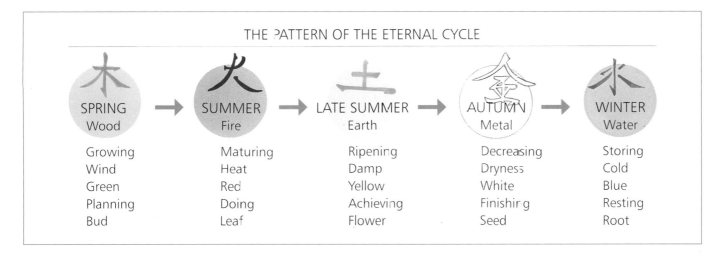

THE PATTERN OF THE ETERNAL CYCLE

SPRING Wood	SUMMER Fire	LATE SUMMER Earth	AUTUMN Metal	WINTER Water
Growing	Maturing	Ripening	Decreasing	Storing
Wind	Heat	Damp	Dryness	Cold
Green	Red	Yellow	White	Blue
Planning	Doing	Achieving	Finishing	Resting
Bud	Leaf	Flower	Seed	Root

Look, it cannot be seen – it is beyond form.
Listen, it cannot be heard – it is beyond sound.
Grasp, it cannot be held – it is intangible.
… The form of the formless,
The image of the imageless.

Tao Te Ching

Returning to practicalities for a moment, if we choose tai chi as our vehicle for the journey, we must naturally first learn the mechanics of the form. It is essential to be thoroughly familiar with these, in order to be able to relax and let go so that the deep and profound benefits of daily practice can be felt. This should be obvious, for how can you relax your mind during your form if you are constantly thinking of what comes next? It simply does not work. Moreover, the patience and dedication required for the learning of the form are qualities that are worth developing in any case, for they hold the key to many of life's successes.

When the movements of the tai chi form have been thoroughly assimilated another very interesting phenomenon arises: this is the quality of stillness. Stillness in the midst of movement is a difficult concept to grasp, and even more difficult to achieve. One way of understanding it, however, is by the practice of stillness itself which can be done as a completely separate exercise to the tai chi form.

The Importance of Stillness

A closely allied practice to that which we have been studying in this book, and in fact one that is often incorporated in the daily practice routine of tai chi, is the even older discipline of *chi kung* (sometimes written as *Qi Gong*). Chi kung means "control or mastery of the breath." There are hundreds of different varieties of chi kung exercises, some based on repetitive movement and some built around fixed positions. In all cases, emphasis is placed on relaxation, on contemplation of the breath, which is deep and regular, and on visualizing the circulation of chi through the body and limbs. Here, we are going to look at six separate chi kung positions – exercises without movement yet which are still especially relevant to tai chi practice. Normally, the time to do these is either just before or directly after your form, although they can be done at any time and in any combination with equally good effect.

Chi Kung Exercises

In each of these exercises, the legs and feet are in the same position – that is, with the feet just a little over shoulder-width apart, and parallel. The legs should have soft knees and a rounded appearance, much like sitting on a horse, while the base of the spine is gently tucked in, as is the chin, so that the whole of the spinal column, including the neck, appears to lengthen. The point of suspension at the crown of the head is visualized – the traditional golden thread going up to the sky by which the body is suspended, totally upright and relaxed. The breath, meanwhile, is directed downward into the abdomen, so that with each in-breath the abdomen expands slightly outward. This makes space for the diaphragm to descend and so allows the air to enter the lungs more easily. Make sure you breathe naturally, however; do not force your breathing. As always, stick to your own natural rhythm and inclinations.

In each of the chi kung positions featured on the following pages, the arms are held out from the body with a pleasing roundness to their shape; there should be no sharp angles at the elbows or wrists. To facilitate the flow of chi around the body, allow the tip of your tongue to rest very gently against the roof of your mouth; this connects the major energy channels that run down the front and up the back of the body. It does not matter if your mouth opens a little because of this, but try to keep breathing in through your nose. Each of these exercises is in fact relevant to one or

(text continues on page 138)

CHI KUNG POSITION ONE

Left. *In the first position the arms are held out in a rounded fashion, as if embracing a tree. Imagine your vital energy flowing around the midline of your body, up the spine and down along the inside of the arms. Use this stance, for example, to contemplate the energy flow in the left arm during the Ward Off (see page 26) or just before the final stage of the Single Whip (see page 30).*

CHI KUNG POSITION TWO

Above. *The second position merely requires that you lower the arms to about the level of the Tan Tien (see page 16). Keep the roundness in your arms and allow your palms to turn slightly upward-facing. Then visualize your vital energy flowing down and into your palms. The overall appearance should look like you are holding a great round bowl. Use this stance to contemplate the energy flow in movements such as Repulse Monkey (see page 53), Wave Hands Like Clouds (see page 58) or, again, the left arm during parts of the Single Whip (see page 30).*

135

CHI KUNG POSITION THREE

Below. *The third position is similar to the first, only this time the palms are turned out. This is a more yang position than the previous two, and your energy is more likely to feel more as if it is projecting outward from the palms. Use it to visualize the energy flow in any of the pushing movements, such as Separate Hands and Push (see page 29) or Release Arm and Push (see page 41). Note how the thumbs are almost horizontal, parallel with the ground.*

CHI KUNG POSITION FOUR

Right. *The fourth position, again, requires that you simply lower the arms down to about the height of the* Tan Tien *(see page 16), bringing your palms down to face the ground. Visualize the energy flowing from the shoulders down into the center of the palms. If you are doing these exercises in series, your legs might begin to tire by this stage, so make sure your knees do not bow inward. Keep sitting on that horse! Use this stance to visualize the energy flow of the left arm in movements such as the final part of Brush Left Knee and Push (see page 36).*

CHI KUNG POSITION FIVE

Left. *In the fifth position the hands are more flattened with the fingers together, and are held with the little-finger side of the hands directed downward. Imagine your energy running from the shoulders along the little-finger side of the arms and into the fingertips – though do make sure there is still space between your elbows and your sides. Use this stance to visualize the energy flow in movements such as Play Guitar* (see page 33), *Fist Under Elbow* (see page 51) *or the early stages of Rollback and Press* (see page 28).

CHI KUNG POSITION SIX

Above. *The sixth and final position simply requires that you turn your hands over and relax the fingers. With both hands now in a typical yin shape, think of energy coming in through the fingertips, or of the fingers themselves growing in length. Use this stance to visualize the energy flow in movements such as the in-breath stage of Pat the Horse* (see page 66), *the Opening* (see page 23) *or the early stages of the Single Whip* (see page 30).

137

more of the tai chi movements. It may only be one arm, or both – but there is always an echo of the form itself.

Throughout these exercises, your mind should be focused on the cycle of the breath and on the cyclical movements of energy around the body – rising up the spine, along the arms, or over the head and down the front of the body back to the *Tan Tien*. And try to disregard any feelings of impatience or discomfort. Those who specialize in chi kung often hold these positions for ten or fifteen minutes at a time, although as an adjunct to tai chi practice, just a few minutes are quite sufficient. Remember, too, that you do not need to do all the exercises together in series. Just explore each one occasionally at the beginning or end of your tai chi session; hold the stance for as long as is comfortable, looking – without effort – for that point of stillness within, and see how you feel. Bear in mind that chi kung, like tai chi itself, is as much about using the mind as it is about using the body.

Returning is the motion of the Tao.
Yielding is the way of the Tao.
The ten thousand things are born of being.
Being is born of non-being.

Tao Te Ching

The Journey Continues

Although a book of this kind is a good introduction to learning tai chi, eventually you may well wish to locate someone who can demonstrate the movements, correct your form if necessary and perhaps even impart to you some of the spirit of tai chi itself.

There are many places where you can study tai chi these days (advice on finding a school or teacher is given on page 141). Most towns have their own adult education centers and perhaps a university or college campus. Tai chi is also being incorporated as a teaching tool in some physical therapy programs. In fact, it can crop up almost anywhere: it is used in drama training, at vacation resorts, in acupuncture colleges and on board ocean liners; it appears in homes for the elderly, in hospital rehabilitation units, in dance studios, and in educational institutes to help those with learning difficulties – anywhere where people are looking for a means of developing relaxation, balance and a sense of harmony between body and mind.

So how do you know if the kind of tai chi you are being taught is the right kind for you? Simple: look for the harmony of yin and yang! There are many ways in which your teacher can demonstrate a knowledge of yin and yang. He or she may be a superb martial artist, for instance, able to use the forces of retreat and attack, yielding and advancing, to stunning effect. Or perhaps the instructor might be a medical practitioner, skilled in the diagnosis of disease using the principles of oriental medicine. Or your teacher might simply be a strong and vibrant personality who is able to display a combination of both sympathy and authority in the method of teaching.

In the world of tai chi, this understanding of the interplay of yin and yang is paramount, and those teachers in whom it is lacking will only be able to go through the motions in a rather mechanical way. It may work for them, and it may work for you – but only up to a point. Thereafter, it will always have its limitations and will only be able to take you so far in your journey.

Practice

It may be a tough message, but even with the best teacher in the world, without regular practice it is impossible to gain the numerous benefits that tai chi can offer. There are no shortcuts in the learning process, either. A good instructor will help you to minimize the amount of time required in the "classroom," but the rest is up to you. Daily practice is best – in fact, without it the mind often tends to forget what has been learned, resulting in an erratic progress in which for every advantage you gain, for every step forward, there is yet another step back. In the end, the tai chi goes nowhere, and neither do you.

Try, therefore, to set aside a little time for yourself each day, ideally around ten to fifteen minutes if you can. Some people may protest that this is unfeasible, but really it only means getting out of bed a little earlier than usual, or perhaps finding a space in the evening or at lunchtime when you would be doing other things anyway. Ultimately, it all comes down to weighing the advantages of different activities within your daily routine and then setting your own priorities. Will you benefit more, for example, from watching the news on television again before you go to bed, or by relaxing your body and illuminating your mind a little by doing some tai chi?

When you practice, try to make sure you will not be disturbed. Naturally, this may not always be easy if you are sharing space with others, but it is best not to be secretive. Tell people what you are doing – even show them if they are curious – and don't be put off if their initial reaction is somewhat less than encouraging. People like to poke fun at others who are trying to improve themselves. They will soon get used to it, however, and once they start to notice the positive changes in you that tai chi can bring, it is more than likely that they will become thoroughly supportive.

In the West people tend to be rather reticent and wary of displaying themselves. And although outdoor practice is best, in the fresh air where there is an abundance of chi, beginners do not

In China, tai chi practice is part of the daily routine. And the Chinese have no qualms about practicing in public, as you can see!

always feel confident enough to do tai chi outdoors – even in their own backyard! However, do try, once you feel reasonably proficient at the form, to work outdoors. Early in the morning is best, since the parks and open spaces are often busy with people engaged in all manner of curious exercises anyway. Join the club! Get out in the fresh air and do some tai chi warm-ups. Then, when you are satisfied that nobody is staring at you (but what does it matter if they are!), go on to do the form. Breathe! Open your lungs and enjoy the energy and freshness all around you! It really makes a world of difference in how you feel. Groups of tai chi enthusiasts often meet on prearranged dates in parks or even on beaches in order to practise together. Look out for these. They will usually be early in the mornings and at weekends. This is a good way of tracking down local teachers in your area if you have not already found one.

TAI CHI PRACTICE: WHERE, WHEN AND HOW

You will find that it is worth bearing in mind the following recommendations when you practise tai chi. These will help you to gain the maximum benefit from your practice.

- *Mornings and evenings are best.*
- *Fresh air is preferable to being indoors.*
- *Never practice on a full stomach.*
- *Never practice when tired.*
- *Always warm up first.*
- *Always practice in loose, comfortable, clean clothing.*
- *Keep the kidneys, throat and feet warm and dry.*
- *Work for at least ten minutes at a time.*

Meditation

Tai chi is often called a "moving meditation" – and that's exactly what it is. All forms of meditation have the following in common: the breath is rhythmic, the mind is empty and still, and the physical world is, in some sense, transcended. Usually this is only accomplished after a great deal of training and self-discipline, since for most of us it is extremely hard to remain still and quiet long enough for this process to occur.

In many of the more static forms of meditation, one is urged to kneel on the ground or sit with the legs crossed in a lotus position, or upon a chair, and to close the eyes and still the mind. For most of us two minutes can seem like a very long time when attempting such a feat; ten minutes becomes an eternity! And sadly many aspirants to the world of meditation are forced to admit defeat before they have barely begun.

Tai chi is different. Because the body is in motion, and because its nervous, motive energy is taken care of to a certain extent by the slow, cyclical movements of the form, the mind is able to wind down and eventually switch off and let go of the endless internal dialogue of mental chatter with which it is normally filled. This, of course, can only be achieved once the movements themselves have become so familiar that they no longer require any conscious effort to perform – so that the tai chi just happens, by itself. The slow, repetitive rhythm of the breath combined with the ebb and flow of the movements becomes your guide to inner quiet; the threshold of meditation is reached, and then … you can simply let go. It is precisely this "letting go" that is at the heart of all meditative and mystical experience.

There is one curious feature to meditation, however. You should never be aware of doing it! Once you cross over the boundary into the meditative state, there is, by definition, no longer any conscious thought. And the moment you think to yourself, "Oh good, I'm sure I'm meditating now!" you are not! You have drifted back into the world of conscious thought. Meditation, like the Tao itself, is without thought.

Simply Being

Once we have reached the stage of moving meditation, the journey of tai chi ultimately takes us to a space that is both deeply internal and yet also universal. This may seem like a contradiction in terms, but the further we can go toward the inner meditative experience, the more vast our horizons become. People often travel to broaden the mind; some have an overwhelming urge to constantly revitalize their lives with fresh experiences, new faces, new places. This is fine, but it may also be doing things the hard way.

In the pursuit of learning, every day something is acquired.
In the pursuit of Tao, every day something is dropped.

Tao Te Ching

This was known, and is still known, by all those who retreat from the world in order to focus on the inner experience. It is the guiding principle behind monastic orders of all cultures and ages. Of course, this can always be taken to extremes and lead to dullness – a contraction of the mind rather than an expansion of it. We all need to experience the real world out there, and embrace it with enthusiasm and courage at every opportunity. But in so doing we also must not neglect the inner self, for this is where the learning process and evolution ultimately takes place.

In the end both types of experience are valid, so that a combination of the two becomes, once again, a state of harmony between the forces of yang and yin – the yang experience of outward exploration tempered by the yin experience of inner contemplation. Blend them together in a life that is rich and rewarding on all levels, and let the adventure begin! Above all recognize that in the eternal cycle that is tai chi, you have met with something greater than yourself. Be at peace with this understanding, and then set about finding a way to let this great impulse enter your life and change it for the better.

Resources

FINDING A TEACHER

To the aspiring student of tai chi, the search for suitable instruction can often develop into something of an eternal quest – a path which becomes, the higher one ventures, ever more mysterious, inscrutable – and *expensive*. It is also notoriously competitive, featuring numerous different styles whose exponents do sometimes try, but usually fail, to reconcile themselves to one another. The result is a rather pleasant and refreshing anarchy, with still no genuinely international or even, to the author's knowledge, national organization representing the whole of the subject, despite the impressive titles that such organizations might employ.

Most people who study tai chi seriously, however, will want to contact a class or group sooner or later in order to progress and to have their tai chi checked over by a more experienced individual. The following routes are suggested.

LOCAL CLASSES

For inexpensive and usually quite adequate introductory classes, try your local adult learning or education center, as well as any local sports or leisure centers in your area. These will be listed in your local phone directory or can be found through your local library.

ESTABLISHED, NATIONAL-BASED TAI CHI SCHOOLS

These usually revolve around the work of one prominent master or teacher and will provide good quality instruction to those who show a genuine interest and are willing to practice on a regular basis. They can be found in the phone directory of capital cities or through advertisements in leading health and fitness magazines.

PRIVATE CLASSES

Smaller organizations or even single teachers working in the field of oriental medicine – of which there are a good many, including the author of this book – can be located through the local press or, again, via advertisements in health and fitness magazines. Some may also run classes at adult learning or education centers or through any number of arts or therapy organizations. For example:

Lawrence Galante
PO Box 1291
New York, NY 10009
USA

Please enclose a stamped, addressed envelope with your enquiry.

If you are particularly interested in the martial arts side of tai chi, look for advertisements in combat or kung fu magazines. Also, most of the more prestigious schools will be keen to train their pupils in martial skills anyway, though this is by no means obligatory.

WHAT TO LOOK OUT FOR ...

Qualifications, if they exist at all, will usually have been awarded within a particular school and will have been bestowed upon loyal pupils who have, in the fullness of time, become instructors themselves. But note: these credentials are not necessarily an insurance of excellence. Rather, the best qualifications to look for in a prospective teacher of tai chi, or any other subject for that matter, are kindness, patience and a willingness to share his or her knowledge with others. If these are lacking, no matter how grandiose the titles, try elsewhere.

In many cultures where wisdom and faith still prevail, there is a saying to the effect that when the pupil is ready, the teacher will appear. Be open to that idea. It is a very profound one, and you will find that it is not without foundation.

SUGGESTED READING

Man-ch'ing, Cheng, *Cheng Tzu's Thirteen Treatise on Tai Chi Ch'uan.* Berkeley, California: North Atlantic Books, 1985.
This book was written by the founder of the short yang form and features excellent photographs of the Master, plus his own meditations on tai chi and Taoism.

Feng, Gia-Fu and English, Jane (trans.), *Tao Te Ching* (Lao Tsu). London: Wildwood House, 1973.
The ancient Chinese classic particularly well translated but with the added bonus of some stunning nature photography.

Galante, Lawrence, *Tai Chi: The Supreme Ultimate.* York Beach, Maine: Samuel Weiser, Inc., 1982.
Action-packed photography accompanies a text written with knowledge and authority by a first-generation pupil of Master Cheng Man-ch'ing.

Hass, E. M., *Staying Healthy with the Seasons.* California: Celestial Arts, 1981.
This is one of the best all-round introductions to the principles of oriental healing.

Klein, Bob, *Movements of Magic.* California: Newcastle Publishing Company, 1984.
An inspiring journey through the world of tai chi by one of America's leading teachers, also a zoologist.

Wing, R. L., *The Illustrated I Ching.* London Aquarian Press, 1987.
A simple and attractive introduction to the ancient classic of divination and inner knowledge.

Parry, Robert, *Tai Chi.* London: Hodder & Stoughton (Headway Lifeguides), 1994.
Features the author performing the short yang form with additional chapters on Taoism and health.

AUDIO/VISUAL

If you would like details of video and audio cassettes by Robert Parry or news of occasional workshops or residential classes on tai chi and related subjects, please write with a stamped, addressed envelope or International Reply Coupon to the address below:

Robert Parry School of Tai Chi and Body Energetics
PO Box 110, Faversham
Kent ME13 9QA
England

Index

Acknowledgements

I would like to take this opportunity to thank all those who have helped make this book possible – thanks firstly to my friends and fellow students Georgina French and Angus McLewin for agreeing to model for the photographs and for taking upon themselves the most difficult task of demonstrating in still photography what is fundamentally a subject of pure motion. Thanks, also, to our photographer Laura Wickenden and everyone at the Paul Forrester studio for their hospitality and expertise and to the Dawes family – Mary, Lesley and Sandys – for allowing us to work in the beautiful setting of their gardens at Mount Ephraim in Kent. I would also like to thank my teachers – near and far – not only from the world of tai chi, but also those involved in chi kung, yoga, shiatsu, acupuncture and oriental medicine, for sharing their knowledge in a spirit of such generosity. Thanks, also, to my very first instructors of all, my parents – in whatever strange and hidden sphere you now reside – and to my partner Ruby for her love and for the most supportive company anyone could possibly ever wish for in another person. Thank you Teresa Chris for your determination; thanks to Peter Smith for your encouragement. And then last, but by no means least, thanks to all the team at Eddison Sadd who have patiently assisted in bringing to press my sometimes very personal vision of tai chi – a truly vast and inexhaustible area of study that most of us poor mortals can only aspire to with an imperfect and incomplete understanding.

EDDISON·SADD EDITIONS

Project Editor Zoë Hughes
Editor Tessa Monina
Proofreader Pat Pierce
Indexer Dorothy Frame

Art Director Elaine Partington
Designer Rachel Kirkland
Illustrators Aziz Khan and
Anthony Duke

Production Hazel Kirkman and
Charles James

The photograph on page 139 is reproduced by kind permission of Mark Henley/Impact.